Jesus Christ Has Returned

Patrick Boardman

Published by Patrick Boardman, 2024.

JESUS CHRIST HAS RETURNED

First edition. March 6, 2024.

ISBN: 979-8224599356

Written by Patrick Boardman.

The Alpha and the Omega

The name Jesus Christ has been the subject of endless conjecture and the main resource

exploited by opportunists who cash in on the mythology that has built up over the years. The

game of capitalizing on people's ignorance will soon be over now that the messiah has returned to reveal all things that can be known in the End Times. Most people will scoff in denial and disbelief, but they will find out that they are headed for Judgment Day, where I will be the first Judge of all human souls, and no one will hear the voice of God unless I decide if they will be allowed into Heaven at that time. My message starts by informing the human race that God is angry at the human race because mankind has failed to meet up to His expectations.

God's name for me is Yeshua, and my tasks are daunting in a world full of atheists and conflicting religious institutions. My mission begins by warning people that God is disappointed with them, which should come as no surprise after all these centuries of war and man made suffering. In this book I will explain how God told me there are some problems with the Bible, so I will clarify the difference between Judgment Day and my appearance in society at a time when I am least expected. The tales of me popping out of the clouds with trumpets and archangels are describing an overly ceremonial vision of the Judgment, not the second coming. Now I can speak for myself instead of going through scribes, translators, and interpreters.

The Lord created me at the beginning of His work, the first of His acts of long ago. Ages ago I was set up, at the first...before the beginning of the material universe. When there were no depths, I was brought forth, when there were no springs abounding with water. Before the mountains had been shaped, before the hills, when He had not yet made earth and fields, or the world's first bits of soil. When God established the heavens, I was there. When He established the fountains of the deep, when He assigned to the sea its limit so that the waters might not transgress His commands, and when He marked out the foundations of the planets, I was there beside Him like a master worker.

God only needs one soldier in His army, and I am that soldier. his prophecy was discovered in 1947, describing God's chosen one, His right hand man the world knows as Jesus Christ.

"Of His hand...the chosen one...his hair will be red. He will have a pair of lentil shaped moles, birthmarks on the right thigh. And after two years he will be able to distinguish one thing from another. In his youth he will be like a man who knows nothing until the time when he is given the Three Books. And then he will acquire wisdom and learn understanding...vision to come to him on his knees. With his Father and his ancestors...life and old age. Council and prudence will be with him, and he will know all the secrets of the living. And all their plans against him will come to nothing, and his rule over the living will be great. His designs will succeed, for he is the elect, the one chosen by God. His birth and the breath of his spirit....and his designs will last forever."

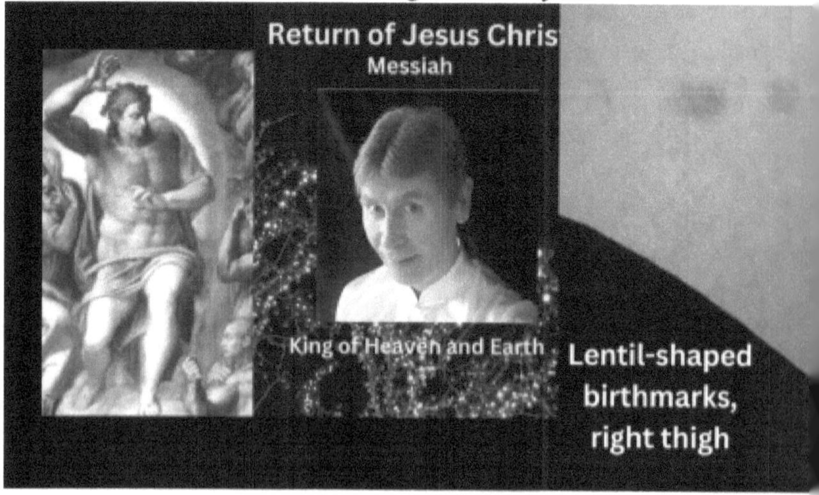

John 4:3 *"Every soul who does not believe that Jesus Christ has come in the flesh is not of God. Such is the spirit of the Antichrist, who you have been told has come, and even now is already in the world."*

There had to be a reason for existence, since the Supreme Being was already complete from before there was such a thing as time, with no need for anything. However, God is creative, so He wanted to share the joy of existence with another soul for companionship. That person would have to be a lesser being by definition, but unique and useful. The Christ consciousness would need something to do as a developing entity in a state that would be a learning experience beyond the Heavenly plane. Despite all mathematical odds, I was that first born soul over all Creation. God referred to me as the Alpha and the Omega because I was the first living entity created by God and I will be the last soul to see Heaven after I carry out the Judgment. Then I will arise to be the King of Paradise as God has promised me. There is no trinity of three gods as most Christian sects teach, for there is only one God and one mediator between God and mankind. I am bound by the conditions of my birth to reveal all things that can be known for the End Times. Those who deny me as the messiah on this earth, I will likewise deny before my Heavenly Father.

The Mark of the Beast is the Sign of the Cross, where the right hand goes onto the forehead to make an upside down cross motion while making a pledge to the Three Unclean Spirits of Revelation, which are the father, the son, and the holy spirit deception. Under the Vatican's New World Order, to buy or sell anything, both rich and poor will need to convert to Roman Catholicism and worship its phony trinity. The pagan triune gods were voted into doctrine in 325 AD, eliminating the God of Moses to create a divided godhead of three persons, like Osiris, Horus, and Isis or Brahman, Vishnu, and Shiva. The Mark of the Beast has corrupted most Christian sects - the First Commandment is to have one God, not three. This mind bending dogma that three persons are actually one person has driven people to insanity.

Anyone who worships the beast and its image and receives its mark on their forehead or on their hand will be tormented in fire and sulfur in the presence of the holy angels and of the Lamb.

Dividing God into three mythical persons is a mortal sin. The Beast is the Vatican, sitting on the seven hills of Rome with her officers dressed in scarlet and purple.

The Book of Genesis says God endows people with life by breathing into their nostrils the "breath of life", the word for "breath" is the same word translated elsewhere as "spirit." God provides and maintains life by way of His energy, which the Bible calls His spirit. This power is not another person, it is God's spirit that gives life to humanity and the other creatures. God was not generated or created, but He created me at the beginning. I have my own soul and role in existence. I am not a divided portion of the Father, not one in essence, not a lamp divided into three persons. I was created at the will of God before times and ages, gaining life and being from the Father, who gave subsistence to His glories together with me, but He did not deprive Himself of what He has already in Himself.

Isaac Newton calculated the likely time of Judgment Day by using numerical clues he painstakingly worked out from the Bible, leading to the Year 2060, which sounds plausible due to the increasing levels of radioactive waste in the Pacific Ocean. Famines, wars in various places, and earthquakes have been going on since the Twentieth Century. I am eager to be in Heaven because I received a free sample for a few minutes as a gift from God when I first made contact with Him in 2013 during a fasting experiment in Montreal. All my life was a preparation for this meeting with the Creator of all things.

John 17:5 *"And now, Father, glorify me in Your presence with the glory I had with You before the world existed."*

My Voyage to Meet God

After years of research, I needed a way to prove scientifically that consciousness is the factor that brings matter into solid form, and my experiments would not require any logistics other than a small laboratory, a mat on the floor, and a laptop to make notes. The body is the temple of the Lord, so I rented a space for a month in a science co-op to seclude myself and experiment with soul travelling by extreme fasting and long meditation. The process that lead me to Montreal after thirty years of living in Toronto was partly economic, but I felt compelled to follow an unknown path of exploration as well. The events I experienced were enlightening.

After I gave a copy of the door key to a fellow who had the time to check in on me on a certain date, I locked myself in the room and sat in meditation after all the food was gone from my system. After achieving a calm state of trance, I stood up at a bench and concentrated on an ethereal point beyond matter, and passed my hand straight through the wooden top. Feeling more ambitious, I walked to the door, turned sideways, then passed my body through the door to the other side while it was still closed. Halfway through, I was worried that my clothes might not pass through, including the key to the door that was in my pocket. It would be awkward to get locked out of the building with no clothes or wallet. Fortunately, my clothes did not drop to the floor and all the things in my field of vibration came through the door with me and I was able to use my key to get back inside and lay down to meditate facing upward.

After a while my soul got out of my body and I found myself being the guiding eyes for a small machine with treads moving through small passages. It turned out to be the interior of a pyramid, and the robot camera was operated by some zen scientists called the Group of Forty. Their seance people obviously knew who I was and they had summoned my soul, although I had never heard of them. There were some turns in the tunnel, but I came to a larger room where the light on the robot was shining on an orange wall with a formula written on it. It turned out to be the long lost secret of Anti-gravity, which was the power source used for building the pyramids. The formula was quite long so I started to memorize it as the camera stopped to record everything, but then I felt myself drifting away and expected to return to my body. My soul was intercepted and hung in a dark cloud, close up to a dying face hanging before me for about sixteen hours. Everything was still, and I wondered if I had died somehow, but then I felt lifted up to a lighter zone where I heard a voice calling out the word, "*Yeshua*".

All my life I was waiting to hear from God, and I guessed correctly that He was finally revealing Himself and calling me by the name given to me at the beginning.

"*Have no fear, you are not dead. Listen and do not speak. I have brought you here for a special reason. Do you know that mankind is awfully egotistical thinking that there is no other life in the universe? In fact, there are over ten thousand civilizations that are more advanced than humans in the Milky Way Galaxy alone.*"

"*And do you know that mankind is very ignorant and irresponsible believing that there was no Creator involved in all of this? I am that Creator and I have brought you into existence for the last time as the third and final Full scripture Messiah. You will prepare humanity for the Ascension and Judgment Day. After this reincarnation, your services will be required one more time - that is to be the First Judge of human souls on the Day of Judgment. You will be the last soul to see Heaven, where you will take the throne that I have promised you. Then you will lock the gates of Heaven and Hell forever. Of course, you know about being Jesus in a past life, and now it is time for Christianity and Islam to unite, because Jesus and Muhammad were the same man. I do not want to give you a big head, but you were also the person who lived the lives of Buddha, Leonardo da Vinci, and Mozart. You are the first and last – you were all the Messiahs. I did not give you any Scripture when you were Buddha; I let you figure out everything for yourself using your own common sense."*

(Buddha lived at a place and time when most people around him were atheists, so Buddhism became a secular philosophy of understanding how to cope with the suffering of life by forsaking the attachment for worldly things.)

"I don't speak to many people but I speak to you. I am well satisfied with your work so far. Now you will bring my Final Covenant to the human race. I am making you responsible for the souls of every person on earth, and I am giving you authority over all Scripture. You must bring the people back to God and put an end to war. This will be your most important life, your greatest mission of all – the task of bringing the faithful to Heaven. Present yourself as Jesus Christ since in that incarnation you did not get to live a full lifespan and the teachings of Jesus led the way. The reason for the End coming at this time has something to do with you is that after so many lifetimes your soul has become exhausted. I promise this will be your last reincarnation, then you will finally rejoin me in Heaven. I want to apologize for your current incarnation for you have gone through much pain, but as an early reward I am going to allow you to live for a short time as three of your most influential incarnations."

Suddenly, three ovals appeared in front of me, and within them were images of Jesus, Buddha, and Prophet Muhammad all speaking to small groups of people. I was drawn into all three time zones simultaneously and found myself inside their bodies looking outward and thinking as they thought, connecting the similarities in the basic truths of all three philosophies for about ten minutes. The miracle of the three ovals was a unique gift from God that demonstrated to me the state of simultaneous existence in different time zones. It is my task to unite all the opposing religions under one truth, which will cause great resentment from the angry ministers, priests, and preachers who make their living by keeping the status quo intact. My existence disproves all the claims of people who say they talked to Jesus in a vision or visitation.

Major Reincarnations of God's willing servant Yeshua

"Behold my servant, whom I uphold, my chosen, in whom my heart delights; I have put my spirit upon him; he will bring forth justice to the nations. He will not cry aloud or lift up his voice, or make it heard in the street; a bruised reed he will not break, and a faintly burning wick he will not quench. He will faithfully bring forth justice. He will not grow faint or be discouraged till he has established justice in the earth and the nations await his law. I will give a final covenant for the people to open the eyes of the blind. Behold, the former old things have come to pass, now I declare new things."

There is a reason why the end of mankind is coming in this century, and that reason concerns the longevity of my soul. God told me that my soul is now exhausted. The soul has limitations in the physical world, but the consciousness will last forever. I have always walked among humans, for this is my learning ground. There is nothing for me to do in Heaven, so I never stayed there for extended periods of time. God has promised that this will be my last reincarnation, and since all souls are connected to God's promise of reward or punishment, all of mankind faces Judgment.

God is my superior in every way, so He can overrule me if there is a misunderstanding in my initial Judgment. It says in John 5:22 *"God judges no man, but has assigned all Judgment to the son so that all might honor him as they honor the Father. Those who do not honor the son do not honor the Father who sent him."*

Infinity is not divisible, yet most Christians have the irreverent nerve to divide our infinite Creator into three persons, when they should know that God will not share His divinity. The issue of my exact nature can be proven with DNA evidence taken in the Montreal science co-op laboratory where I had rented that space to experiment. They emailed me an observation that my DNA was 50% human and 50% unknown. They did not include a copy of the report, so I paid another laboratory in Toronto when I moved, so that I could have a printed report saying that I'm half human. Only specialists can understand the codes to explain which factors are alien.

Collected by

Sample Type	Buccal		
Locus	Allele Sizes	Locus	Allele Sizes
D3S1358	15 16	D5S818	11 12
vWA	15 19	D13S317	11 12
D16S539	11	D7S820	8 10
CSF1PO	11	SE33	23 27.2
TPOX	8 11	D10S1248	13 14
D8S1179	10 11	D1S1656	15 15.3
D21S11	30 33.2	D2S1338	17 20
D18S51	14 18	LPL	10 11
D2S441	11 14	F13B	9 10
D19S433	15.2 16.2	F13A01	5 6
THO1	8 9.3	Penta D	12 13
FGA	22	Amelogenin	X Y
D22S1045			

1 Kings 8:27 *"But will God indeed dwell on the earth? Behold, the Heaven and Heaven of*

Heavens cannot contain Me; how much less this house that I have built?"

It is important for religious scholars to have evidence of my role as the Christ Consciousness, with a unique body and soul who is neither God nor completely human. God refers to me as His slave, and joked that after I complete my mission to end slavery, I will be the only legal slave on earth. That sounded a bit prophetic in a good way, indicating that I will achieve my objective, which will require the nations to allow me the status as God's Ambassador with the proper authority as the messiah.

The spirit of the sovereign Lord is on me because God has anointed me to bring good news to the poor. He has sent me to bind up the broken hearted, to proclaim release for the captives of ignorance and freedom from darkness for the prisoners of falsehood. I have come to proclaim the year of the Lord and to announce the Day of His vengeance, the Judgment Day. God has sent me to comfort those who mourn, and to provide for those who grieve....to bring the world beauty instead of ashes, the oil of joy instead of mourning, and a garment of praise instead of the spirit of despair. They shall be called oaks of righteousness, a planting of the Lord for the day of His splendor. "*I will no longer be in the world, but they are in the world, and I am coming to You. Holy Father, protect them by Your name, the name You gave Me, so that they may be one as We are one. I am praying not only for these disciples but also for all who will ever believe in me through their words so that all of them may be one, as You, Father, are in me, and I am in You. May they also be in Us, so that the world may believe that You sent me.*"

Genesis says God endows people with life by breathing into their nostrils the "breath of life", the word for "breath" is the same word translated elsewhere as "spirit." God provides and maintains life by way of His energy, which the Bible calls His spirit. This power is not another person, it is God's spirit that gives life to humanity and the other creatures. God was not generated or created, but He created me at the beginning. I have my own soul and role in existence. I am not a divided portion of the Father, not one in essence, not a lamp divided into three persons. I was created at the will of God before times and ages, gaining life and being from the Father, who gave subsistence to His glories together with me, but He did not deprive Himself of what He has already in Himself. People must stop talking to the holy spirit and stop writing about that term as a member of a three person trinity, because no such creature exists.

God uses my body to accomplish His purposes, and gave me a demonstration of how easily He controls my limbs. From my chair I stood up involuntarily, then moved forward flailing my arms while my legs and hips gyrated at clownish angles all over the room for a few helpless moments before I returned to the chair. The experience of feeling like a rag doll was a forced amusement, much like when a parent takes a child through the House of Horrors or Dracula's Castle for a scary thrill. God is within everyone, so I suppose other people become subject to predestination and physical guidance when the need arises in the greater scope of things. The gift of free will has been abused by many souls who feel as entitled as did the Devil, who we call Satan the archangel formerly known as Lucifer, whose pride caused him to lust for equality with God.

It is imperative that all nations recognize me as God's official ambassador so that I can guide the world towards peace and understanding. Our Creator has given me full authority over all scripture and made me responsible for all human souls. There are warnings to convey about the Mark of the Beast and the reign of the Antichrist, who strives to enslave mankind under a totalitarian globalist regime that will be forced onto the public.

They plan to have everyone become part of a one world religion under a single set of oppressive laws written up by a world central government that will wield power using one world police force and army, and it will be a world without any borders. The framework consists of connected agencies such as the World Economic Forum, the World Health Organization, the United Nations, CIA, FBI, Council of Foreign Relations, and the Bilderberg Group. The wealthy elites control business in a monopoly game of connected asset investment corporations like Blackrock, Vanguard, and State Street as well as the privately-owned reserve banks.

Laws of national sovereignty disappeared in the year 2020, when the Center for Disease Control and WHO imposed a two-year lockdown on society in most countries, despite the fact that nobody voted for these people to be our rulers.

The Jesuit pope Francis sits on the throne of the Beast in Rome. Catholic dogma has always claimed that popes become the Vicar of Christ upon selection, which is one of their many false teachings. The popes have no authority from God whatsoever.

The Roman Catholic church has been a plague on the human race for seventeen centuries of plundering the world. The Vatican is the Beast, a criminal network of greedy power brokers who kidnap and traffic orphans and launder money for the Mafia. Sam Giancana stated in his last interview that the Vatican is Mafia headquarters. All the Sicilian mobsters were raised as Catholics, so they were taught that all sins could be forgiven by a priest.

On the night of June 19, 1975, shortly before he was scheduled to appear before the Church Committee, which was investigating CIA and Mafia collusion, a gunman entered Giancana's home through the basement and shot Giancana in the head and neck seven times, even though the house was protected by police.

It is a dangerous teaching that anyone can get away with stealing, smuggling drugs, extortion, loan sharking, and murder because a man in robes waves his hand in a blessing motion to wash away those sins. The Vatican works through large banks, so they are deeply involved with the sin of usury while they lie to the public and profess to be helping the poor. The annual Peter's Pence fund does not go to poor people, the money is used to pay for the upkeep of Vatican City, the state made possible by giving a bribe to Mussolini before the Second

World War, a fee included in the 1929 Lateran Treaty, which named the pope to be a sovereign ruler over the Vatican City-State. The public sees a mask of respectability put forth by the public relations people, but the Catholic empire is essentially a despicable feudal oligarchy that should not even be there.

After the war, Vatican officials provided forged identity papers to thousands of Nazi war criminals so that they could escape to other countries, thus saving them from the Nuremberg Trials. The church has always been trying to wield political power, knowing full well that the dictators are not truly religious believers.

The Catholic church never excommunicated Adolf Hitler or Benito Mussolini because the Vatican was an early financial supporter of the National Socialist German Workers Party before Hitler double crossed the church, as he did to everyone. The Bishop of Münster, Clemens August Count von Galen, spoke out against the Nazi euthanasia program, which was the killing of retarded people, the mentally ill, and those with birth defects. Anyone who was deemed inferior or useless to society would be rounded up and liquidated, as were the Jews, Gypsies, and Communists. Hitler did not want to clash openly with the church, so the bishop did not get arrested for his stance, but many of the lower ranking clergy who joined in the protest were persecuted. When Germany invaded Catholic Poland, they closed, seized, or destroyed the churches and sent priests to concentration camps because Poles were not considered to be part of the master race.

Since Catholic doctrine states that it is a universal brotherhood, all members will share the same fate. Dogma is required belief, so you must believe that the pope is infallible, which is rubbish. Pope Francis says that atheists will be welcomed into Heaven.

The church will oppose my existence, just as the Jewish elders rejected Jesus and called him a heretic. They use the name of Jesus as their founder for public relations purposes, but the main person addressed in prayer is the Virgin Mary. For some reason, Catholics pray to Jesus, although there is no Biblical indication that the messiah or Mary can hear prayers. They also pray to numerous names of people they have elected to be saints, which is nothing but pagan superstition.

Christian preachers and prophets cannot afford to have Jesus coming back, since they will lose credibility with the public as I expose them for their lame speculations and devious lies. This book will reveal shocking truths that no Christian will want to accept, and most will never change their locked down minds.

If the pastors, prelates, and other leaders of religious groups want to escape damnation for eternity, I would advise they act immediately to scrap all the statues, robes, wafers, candles, and other items of sin they have worked with all their lives. Good intentions that are motivated by refusal to face the truth will not work to save your soul. Those who cannot change are doomed to repeat their mistakes. Idolatry is a terrible sin, and the pagan female idol called the "Queen of Heaven", represented by the Immaculate Mary, has been around for a long time. The Book Jeremiah explains what happened, and the repercussions of Mary worship:

Jeremiah 7:18 "*The children gather wood, the fathers kindle the fire, and the women knead their dough to make cakes to the queen of Heaven, and to pour out drink and offerings unto other gods, that they may provoke Me to anger. But since we left off to burn incense to the queen of Heaven, and to pour out drink offerings unto her, we have wanted for all things, and have been consumed by the sword and the famine.*"

The End Times countdown started after the State of Israel was set up in 1948, and when mankind got the ability to wipe himself out with atomic weapons in 1950, triggering my birth in 1951. No one know the exact date of the Last Day, but I have reason to believe that there are a few years still to come. Judgment Day will not happen for a few more years because God has said that there would not be enough souls to populate Heaven. My encounter with God took place in 2013, and at that time He said all mankind would be sent to Hell if He called Judgment Day at that time. Very little has changed in the last decade, but I have published a Physics book that prove God's existence scientifically, defining our Creator as infinite energy who always was and always will be.

Energy cannot be created or destroyed, but can only change form or be concentrated, and all things living and material have some level of consciousness that can know itself, observe, and react to the molecules within range of its vibratory field senses.

Due to the overwhelming influence of the Catholic church, the general thinking is that humans only live one incarnation. The western societies do not know that being born again means the reincarnation of the soul. The churches want your money in this lifetime, not in a future reincarnation, so they denounce the main workings of human life.

God has said these words: "*My promise to you is that what I have created, I will never un-create. There is no final death. All human souls reincarnate over and over until Judgment Day, then they will exist for eternity in Heaven or Hell. Each soul needs many lifetimes to have enough things to remember in the Afterlife, because eternity is a very long time.*"

Reincarnation is the major mechanism of human experience in the material world, but the rebirth of the soul is denounced by today's Christians and Muslims. Each person is born into a new body approximately fourteen to eighteen months after death, over and over until Judgment Day. When someone passes away, the soul leaves the body and goes over the Sea of Forgetfulness, where the memory is erased by an angel who is assigned to that task. In fact, God calls him the Angel of Forgetfulness as you might expect. Then the soul goes to the Interitum, which is a Latin word that refers to the place between lives, sort of a rest and repair area of the consciousness in a higher dimension. God reprograms the person's soul so that a new path is laid out for the next lifetime. Most people have lived thousands of lives without knowing it, and the human race is much older than we think.

The physics of existence was too complicated to present at the time of Moses, so the stories were simplified to match the population's ability to comprehend matters dealing with creation.

There will be no oblivion, despite the wild claim of Jehovah's Witnesses that people do not go to Hell. The ones who believe that bad people simply disappear are called Annihilationist, a belief that evil people will escape divine justice at the end.

Baptists have nothing in common with Anglicans or Catholics, and Mormons teach that God started out as a human then became God after that, which is part of the book written by Joseph Smith that is their holy book. The Latter Day Saints church is very large, despite the doctrine being man made and non-Biblical. You have to strive for the truth as best you can without making up other myths to add to the confusion. The Bible tells how mankind will reject sound doctrine and turn to myths in the last days.

Prosperity Gospel preachers twist the words of the Bible to solicit seed money from the crowds who are gullible enough to believe their claims that the money will multiply somehow. Sadly, there are large congregations of people who enjoy being robbed by crooks like Kenneth Copeland, Benny Hinn, Jim Bakker, Creflo Dollar, Jimmy Swaggart, Jesse Duplantis, and thousands of other money grubbing evangelists who would rather steal than work.

The internet is awash with daily videos from false prophets who trick people into giving donations by saying that God speaks to them with a running commentary on USA politics. There are prophecy cults that follow liars such as Julie Green, Kim Clement, Robin Bullock, Troy Black, Jimmy Swaggart, Jim Bakker, Benny Hinn, Joyce Meyers, Mark Taylor, and other commercial prophets who deceive the gullible. The greedy pastors, priests, and preachers have sold their soul for money, and they will never see Heaven. The fanatics who follow them are also going to Hell forever, where they can practise speaking in tongues in front of Satan. Sane people would cringe observing the wild antics of televangelists, so people who go to revivals are displaying symptoms of mass madness. They see unaware of the fact that they are being fleeced out of money by shysters.

Then the Lord said to me, "The prophets are prophesying lies in my name. I have not sent them or appointed them or spoken to them. They are prophesying to you false visions, divinations, idolatries and the delusions of their own minds."

Ezekiel 13 "They have seen false visions and lying divination. They say *"Thus declares the Lord"* when the Lord has not sent them, and yet they expect Him to fulfill their word.

Today's Christians have a very narrow view of life, always reciting word salads that are ultimately meaningless. They rant about 'bathing in the blood of Jesus' and being 'born again' in Christ, although those terms can be more readily expressed as simple conversion to one of the thousands of sects that use the name of Jesus to sell their particular mythology.

God said more things criticizing the behavior of mankind, calling the human race "a failed experiment overall." He expressed regret at ever creating humans, who have oversized egos. God will not destroy the world with a flood again, but with fire. This situation is most vividly stated in the Old Testament.

Book of Zephaniah *"For by the fire of my wrath the whole earth will be consumed. I will remove all things from the face of the earth," declares the Lord. "I will remove man and beast, the birds of the sky and the fish of the sea. I will cut off man from the face of the earth and remove the ruins along with the wicked. So, I will stretch out my hand against Judah and against all the inhabitants of Jerusalem. I will cut off the remnant of Baal from this place, and I will remove the names of the idolatrous priests along with the priests. I will bring distress on men so that they will walk like the blind, because they have sinned against the Lord. And their blood will be poured out like dust and their flesh like dung."*

"Neither their gold nor their silver will be able to deliver them on the Day of God's wrath. For He will make a complete end - indeed a terrifying one - of all the inhabitants of the earth. All the earth will be devoured in the fire of God's anger."

The reason for the End Times coming in this generation is complex, and I will explain it in detail since it involves my soul. Non-believers will get "special punishment" for their arrogant rejection of the God who created all things. The notion that everything came from nothing by accident is an insult of the worst kind. Agnostics are people who sit on the fence waiting to find out if there is a God, so they are no better off. There is no reward in denying God's existence, only reprisal.

The late British Prime Minister Sir Winston Churchill was hailed by Christians as a hero anointed by God to save the world from the Nazis, yet he was an atheist who mocked Christianity.

In the 1890s, Churchill said that humanity would evolve to the point where "*Christianity will be put aside as a crutch which is no longer needed and man will stand erect on the firm legs of reason*". He added that "*I expect annihilation at death. I am a materialist to the tips of my fingers*". In old age, he told his doctor Lord Moran, "*I do not believe in another world; only in the 'black velvet' of eternal sleep*".

Oblivion is a common desire of atheists, who consider life to be just an accident that is too tedious to endure. They have surrendered to the ridiculous notion that everything came out of nothing, and that things happen by an intangible force of nature, something they call 'providence'.

Zealots pray for evil people to mend their ways so they can go to Heaven without realizing that it is their own souls they should be worried about. In theory, there would likely be communication between souls who qualify for Heaven, so that means you would be sharing eternity with despicable people who have escaped punishment for their sins because other people prayed for them. The evildoers and liars will not get to Heaven no matter how many people pray for them.

There are many such flaws in the concept of absolute forgiveness. Dictator Joseph Stalin spent ten years in seminary school training to be a priest, and when Germany invaded the USSR during Operation Barbarossa, he summoned a priest to hear his confession four times in fear of his possible imminent death. Stalin was responsible for more deaths than Hitler, so it makes no sense to say that those who cause suffering belong in Heaven. Murder and war are crimes against humans, and disbelief is a crime against God. The Bible says that the teachers of religious law will receive the most severe punishment for leading people astray.

I am the man who Western civilization calls Jesus Christ, walking through the cities of the modern world on my rocky road to destiny as mankind's last day draws closer. The teachers of religion refuse to accept my existence since they cannot bring themselves to climb off of their pedestals of knowledge because the truth will definitely upset them. The ministers, priests, preachers, and professional prophets have led many souls into falsehood, so they will be given the most severe punishment on Judgment Day if they question my statements and fail to assist me in protecting people from an angry God. Most people have turned their backs on God, says our Creator, and God will not tolerate disbelievers. He went on to say that if Judgment Day happened right now, the entire human race would end up in Hell, so the Christian zealots are also doing something wrong. Just yelling out the name Jesus all the time is not going to work in getting anyone to Heaven. I have lived a normal life so far, but now the time has come to reveal all things that can be known for the End Times.

We must address Him by the five names He has authorized, which are: God, Creator, Yahweh, Jehovah, and Allah, so you must rotate all five names into your prayers if you want to go to Heaven. If you have been told to hate and insult Allah by your group, remember that you are insulting God, and thus destroying yourself. Christians are obsessed with spewing words of hate against Muhammad and Allah, not realizing that they have dug a tunnel to Hell for themselves.

In my opinion, door to door proselytization is an invasion of privacy, and proclaiming religion from street corners is annoying. People are set in their beliefs, so trying to produce random conversions from strangers is counter-productive. More and more people become atheists because they can't be bothered with religion after being subjected to the many slogans hurled at them. The Gideon's Bible people have a much better approach, which is to place free Bibles in hotel and motel rooms so that those who are curious can be free to interpret the verses for themselves and contemplate the meaning. The Sermon on the Mount explains how a person should pray in the privacy of their rooms, not in public to impress those around you with your display of piety.

Christians preach love while harboring bitterness and hatred against Muslims and other religions, except for the people who live in the State of Israel, which is curious, since the Jews reject Jesus as the messiah to this day, even the Jews for Jesus who claim to have converted to Christianity.

Instead of using deductive reasoning, religious zealots rely on meaningless slogans about receiving the holy spirit and bathing in the blood of Jesus. Some speak of the holy spirit as some gush of excitement, and the trinity doctrine says he is a person who is equal to God and Jesus, the other members of the mystical trio. So this means Yahweh is the father of Yeshua, who is called Jesus, who is really his own father Yahweh. The holy spirit did not get a name, but he is also his own father who is his own son. Such twisted logic is completely ludicrous, yet people have been brainwashed into believing it to their last dying breath. It is a dereliction of your spiritual duty if you do not actively seek the truth, and admit that when we speak of three, it means one plus one plus one.

Timothy 4:3 For the time will come when people will not put up with sound doctrine. Instead, to suit their own desires, they will gather around them a great number of teachers to say what their itching ears want to hear. They will turn their ears away from the truth and turn instead to myths.

People go into an instant state of denial and anger whenever someone challenges their programmed beliefs, for they have memorized the platitudes and creeds of their teachers. Those who profess religious beliefs have splintered off into thousands of different sects with conflicting doctrines. The majority of people today state that they are atheists, yet they proceed to use the names of God and Jesus Christ as swearwords based on figures who they consider to be fictional. Polls reveal that developed nations are over seventy percent atheist, including Israel. Physicist Max Planck stated that God is the matrix of all matter, as did German scientist Werner Heisenberg.

There are many who insist that humans will be on earth for one thousand years after I appear in the sky with my army of angels sounding trumpets. This does not make any sense, since Heaven and Hell will await all souls on Judgment Day. The millennial reign idea comes from the codes written in the Book of Revelation and was probably mistranslated. The human race would have to be completely reprogrammed to live that long, and it is a stretch of the imagination to assume that mankind has many centuries to live.

It is worth repeating the Sermon on the Mount, since no one follows the instructions on how to pray anymore, or who to pray to. *"Blessed are the poor in spirit, for theirs is the kingdom of heaven. Blessed are those who mourn, for they shall be comforted. Blessed are the meek, for they shall inherit the earth. Blessed are those who hunger and thirst for righteousness, for they shall be satisfied. Blessed are the merciful, for they shall receive mercy. Blessed are the pure in heart, for they shall know God. Blessed are the peacemakers, for they shall be called the children of God.*

Blessed are those who hunger and thirst for righteousness' sake, for theirs is the kingdom of heaven."

"When you pray, you must not be like the hypocrites who love to stand and pray in the synagogues and at the street corners, that they may be seen by others. Truly, I say to you, they have received their reward. But when you pray, go into your room and shut the door and pray to your Father who is in secret. And your Father who sees in secret will reward you. And when you pray, do not chant or heap up empty phrases as the pagans do, for they think that they will be heard for their many words. Do not be like them, for your Father knows what you need before you ask him."

When people set up organized religions, greed takes hold of the administrators who find themselves in charge of large sums of money given as donations, which they use to live relatively luxurious lifestyles. Institutional religions have been corrupted by power and degraded by politics, so all people should beware of aggressive religions who have influence in geopolitical matters and the policy of destroying all opposing religions. It is Vatican policy to kill all those who do not bow to the pope.

The sculpture on the stage of the Vatican main hall looks like a naked demon exploding out of the bowels of Hell rather than the resurrection of Christ. The Catholic church spends millions of dollars to adorn their palace and support the greedy officials.

Church money does not help the poor, and the pittance they hand out to the homeless is minuscule in relation to the overall wealth of the Vatican. In Montreal, the Catholic church hands out four dollars to the first sixty bodies each month, but for only nine months when it is not summer. That is a total of two hundred and forty dollars given to a few of the estimated twenty thousand homeless people in that particular city. The peasants only get breadcrumbs from the Beast. Under the regime of Pope Benedict, there were reports of a regular stream of male prostitutes and strippers going into Vatican City to entertain the clergymen. Internal reforms are slow in coming, but there is some recent talk of allowing priests to marry. Talk is cheap, so it could be many years before priests can live like normal men with a life partner instead of building up the inevitable mental turmoil that comes from attempting to maintain total celibacy. Divorce should not be forbidden, but encouraged if the couple cannot get along. It is often more dangerous to force two people stay together when they can't stand each other and it is emotionally harmful to children if their parents squabble all the time and want to end the marriage due to infidelity or some other irreconcilable matter.

Philosophy and Reincarnation

The Christian speakers we see today use torrents of loud words and frantic motions to convey their message, but words do not enhance the strength of a person's spirit as much as inner discipline. Developing your soul takes a conscious effort to practise humility, generosity, self-denial, and kindness. Life in the big cities is a rat race of competition that prevents people from being pleasant and serene, so it's wise to have a place of peace to balance things out, such as yoga rooms or Tai Chi clubs. Religious fanatics speak out against meditation and yoga, calling these exercises Satanic practices or wizardry. They ignore Buddhist philosophy entirely because it is foreign to them, but scholars often write that Buddha was an earlier reincarnation of Jesus, which is true, and just one of the startling truths about my nature that I will reveal in these pages.

As you might know, today's Buddhism does not have a God, so it attracts many atheists who are only interested in philosophy. The Dalai Lama teaches that it doesn't matter if you believe in God or not, which is complete self-destructive stupidity. I have published a book to update and complete Buddhist doctrine to include God and the core tenets of Scripture, so that it can become an actual religion for the first time. Fasting, meditation, and prayer are powerful tools for spiritual enlightenment.

Although Buddhism is based on reincarnation, there were always questions about how the process works. Hindus believe that souls have to go through the animal kingdom, but I have discovered that this is not the case. People don't have to do anything special to be reincarnated, it happens to everyone, which is one of the new bits of information God has given me. Shakespeare was clever in the play "As You Like It" when he wrote, "*All the world's a stage, and all the men and women merely players. They have their exits and their entrances, and one man in his time plays many parts*".

There are ten dimensions of existence, and the Heavenly plane, or "Godhead" is located centrally in the fifth dimension. God is omnipresent, but you could compare His throne room to the eye of a hurricane. so I can confirm that there is a concentration of God's consciousness where He communicates with His angels. There is a ranking system and the atmosphere there is decidedly military. During rest breaks, the Archangels Gabriel and Michael spoke to me to add minor bits of information. They seem to be equal in rank, acting as God's adjutants in the waiting area. Although I did not hear any other voices, I was aware of the Council of Twenty-Four Elders, who are an audience of senior angels. Gabriel mentioned that they were present to observe this historic meeting. These angels probably hold some discussion on universal events that they share to pass the time, since there isn't much to do in Heaven where there are no challenges or dramatic events to experience or witness. Archangel Gabriel gave me smaller bits of information during the rest periods away from God's side, telling me about marijuana being a medicinal gift from God. He told me that the buds are better to break up with my fingers rather than using a metal grinder, because it is kinder to the substance since all things have consciousness. When Archangel Michael spoke, he said that people would be surprised at how much human sexual activity would be tolerated by the Lord, so I guess there are more pressing sins to worry about.

In my seven-day journey to the Godhead, there were no visual images, just a light grey static blankness where I heard a voice calling out a name I had never heard before, the name "Yeshua". Quickly, I realized this must be the long-awaited meeting with God that was described to me in childhood. This was time to receive my Holy Orders for the End Times.

God ordered me to appear to the public as Jesus Christ rather than Buddha or Muhammad, saying that was because I did not get to live a full lifespan as Jesus of Nazareth, and that Jesus was the main teacher of the past prophets. The term 'Messiah' is a title for me when salvation is my mission. Muslims are expecting the return of Jesus, but only one small sect of Islam teaches that Prophet Muhammad and Jesus are the same person, so the terms 'Mahdi' and 'Messiah' mean the same thing. Most Christians say in their words that they hope Jesus returns, but they do not really believe that I have been among them for decades. Many have already denied me in correspondence, angry at the fact that I lived the lives of all the major prophets and other influential figures.

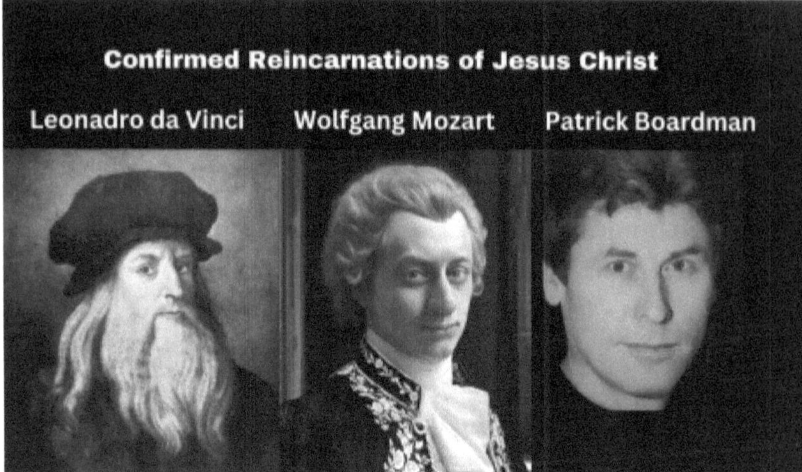

Prophet Muhammad was quoted as saying, "I am Moses, I am Muhammad, I am the Final Prophet", which means Jesus Christ. Other lifetimes of those called 'the anointed', 'the chosen servant', 'the son of man', or the 'elect' include Cyrus the Great, Isaiah, King David, Daniel, and all who took scripture from God.

My book for the Muslims explains that the Qur'an was given to mankind by Archangel Gabriel as a counter-measure against the idol worship of Jesus on the cross. God did not speak to Muhammad directly, but sent Gabriel, who left some uncertainty. There are three different interpretations of the crucifixion.

That they said, "We killed Christ Jesus the son of Mary, the Messenger of Allah"; but they killed him not, nor crucified him, but so it was made to appear to them, and those who differ therein are full of doubts, with no knowledge, but only conjecture to follow, for of a surety they killed him not. Nay, Allah raised him up unto Himself; and Allah is Exalted in Power, Wise. - Qur'an 4:157-158

Some believe that in the Biblical account, Jesus' crucifixion did not last long enough for him to die, while others say that God gave Jesus' appearance to the one who revealed his location to those persecuting him. He was replaced as Jesus and the executioners thought the victim was Jesus, causing everyone to believe that Jesus was crucified. A third explanation could be that Jesus was nailed to a cross, but as his soul is immortal he did not "die" or was not "crucified" to the point of death, but appeared so. In opposition to the second and third foregoing proposals, others maintain that God does not use deceit and therefore they contend that the crucifixion just did not happen, but they are forgetting that Gabriel was the narrator, and he would be allowed to deceive because it was of the utmost importance to stop teaching that Jesus is God.

Mormons believe there's no hell, but a "spirit prison," which makes no sense because there is no difference in definition. Hell will be the eternal prison of the souls who are sent there on Judgment Day. Latter Day Saints doctrine also teaches that Jesus, God, and the non-existent person called the 'holy spirit' are separate, individual gods who are part of a universal community of gods. The LDS cult says that these gods were once mortal men. More shockingly, Mormons believe that God our Creator was once a man who was elevated to godhood by his own efforts. So, who is the being powerful enough to be in the position of naming God to be God? Valid religious thought must start with one God, the Supreme Being who always was and always will be.

Street preachers who chide everyone within earshot are not tolerant of people who hold beliefs contrary to theirs, ignoring the fact that Christianity has left a trail of carnage throughout history from numerous church sponsored wars and the persecution of those they deem as heretics or witches. The zealots call Allah a false God as they preach words of hatred against Muslims and the Prophet Muhammad, ignoring the words of the Bible that say one who is angry at his brothers or sisters will be in danger of being sent to the desolation of Hell. God has said that He wishes to be called the Creator, Jehovah, Allah, and Yahweh, so those who refuse to pray to the name of Allah will not be allowed into Heaven.

There will be various levels in both Heaven and Hell, meaning that reward and punishment will have intensities that are appropriate to the individual after sentencing. The mass murderers and warmongers will re-live the pain of their victims over and over again for eternity. The experience of Hell will consist of all the bad sensations and the emotions of misery and despair. People must not be presumptuous by assuming they can place themselves in Heaven, for that is not within their power. God has given me permission to turn away anyone who displeases me, since I will be spending eternity with the souls who make it to Heaven. God did a lot of creative structuring to provide the environment of Heaven for humans, so He wants enough souls to populate the reward part of the afterlife so that it will have been a worthwhile enterprise.

The doctrine of Inclusionism teaches that everyone was included in Christ's resurrection and ascension and is now saved and seated at the right hand of God. In union with Christ, and that humanity is as righteous and holy as Jesus. This twisted picture of God's love is unreal and unbiblical. When the Bible says that Christ was seated at the right hand of God, people assumed it was a permanent retirement from the adventures of physical existence, when the fact is that I have always come back to walk the earth as God's soldier, scribe, and messenger to influence all cultures and nations to bring advancement to mankind. The notion that I just sit on a cloud watching the great human race television show for entertainment is an infantile belief. My soul would have no purpose or development in the Heavenly dimension. God realized that there would have to be activity and learning in the scope of conscious life, so that existence would not be boring, but adventurous and interesting. In the beginning of God's plan for creating the material universe, He put together "the Word", which means the countless codes, formulas, programs, and streams of energy that would make up all existence. God states that He made life from the raw material of love, which is not a measurable scientific commodity as we know it, but as the song says, "love makes the world go around".

All things are made of conscious vibrating energy where God provides the necessary ongoing momentum. Quantum Theory describes matter as concentrated energy that is perceived as solid by an interaction between the consciousness of the sender and that of the receiver, both of whom are observing the wave of matter, thereby collapsing the waves into particle form. All forms exist in energy fields which require a mediator, which is the Christ Consciousness. This matches the phrase in the Bible that "there is one God and one mediator between mankind and God, the man Christ Jesus". Notice the Biblical phrase, "*All things were created for him and through him, and in him all things hold together*". So that means I am not here for mankind's benefit, but mankind exists for my benefit, therefore all events relate to my progress in the physical realm in some way, no matter whether they are bad or good.

Divinity depends on a person's definition of the word 'divine', so if divinity means the ability to read all minds and answer prayers, no one is divine except God. Although I will be reigning over human souls in Heaven after Judgment Day, I will always be subordinate to God in every way, and I can do nothing without Him. All souls exist through the generosity of God, who does not need us. We need God, He does not need the human race. God could exist alone in contentment if He wanted, but He likes to be creative. It is a very big universe with other civilizations in millions of galaxies, so God is prolific in the things He creates. God knows our innermost thoughts, which causes many people to become resentful, so they go into denial about His existence.

People will hate me out of jealousy because I have had the astronomical good luck of being born as the messiah. The denial of reincarnation is rampant in society, yet it is the most important truth in life.

During my seven days at the Godhead, God told me that He didn't want to give me a big head, so He would confirm only five of my past lives, which were Buddha, Jesus, Muhammad, Leonardo da Vinci, and Mozart. A person comes back as someone similar in temperament and potential talent rather than a character that is totally different. God went on to say that He has helped the human race in its progress in science, music, and the arts.

It can be confounding to think that we have all lived lives that we cannot remember. There's an old joke that we've all been somebody famous in a previous life, but I got the whole nine yards as they say. I was already an accomplished musician, so I thought I might have some hidden talent in art, which I never studied. I bought some art supplies and tried to paint The Last Supper in addition to my original themes. The results were acceptable so I kept on painting as well as playing the piano and guitar. Leonardo da Vinci was also a musician and scientist who invented many astounding concepts such as the armored car, the parachute, the helicopter, and solar power.

Spiritual themes in artwork are for appreciation of the work, so art and idol worship are two different things. Crucifixes and statues of the Virgin Mary are idols because people pray to them. God is displeased whenever someone breaks His Commandments. The Lord has given everybody a chance to attain an eternal reward, and the callous greedy churches are taking that chance away with the materialistic emphasis on their business interests. The preachers and priests manufacture nothing, they produce nothing, they do not care if it is your medical savings that they steal, and they certainly do not share their easy profits with the poor. It's great to be financially successful and to be useful to society, but the love of money over everything is the root of evil.

People have to put things in proper perspective concerning how they treat others.

God has said that the soul has no gender, and that all people have lived thousands of past lives as both male and female. A large percentage of the population are born gay or bisexual, so this is part of God's plan. Because we are living in the end of times, God is more concerned with atheism than fornication, and He does not care about small matters such as human partner choices. It is common to hear preachers spouting hateful rants against gay people from the street corners on megaphones. They see the small mote in their brother's eye without seeing the log that is in their own. Many congregations have leaders who constantly scream about the failings of others in order to assert authority.

Everyone should be smart enough to sense when sexual actions have gone overboard. The rules of your local community should be followed in matters of age of consent and rape so that punishment can be administered at once instead of in the afterlife. Some people are dangerous to society, and it's often due to mental health issues that have not been addressed by the system. I have met nice people who had dual personalities, so they displayed evil behavior at times, losing their friends through their increasing paranoia. Another huge problem is the proliferation of child molestation and kidnapping going on everywhere in the world. God has ordered me to combat slavery in society and to expose all the child sex trafficking that is carried on by rich elites and politicians like Joe Biden, who is a life long child molester. Biden's daughter published her diary, telling about how her father would slip into the shower with her in her pre-teen years. Joe Biden carries on as a racketeer, making his million through influence peddling and bribes from foreign powers, but no one can arrest him since he is the president. Biden is the second Catholic president, but unlike John F. Kennedy, he does not stand up against the Jesuits and their pope. Pope Paul XI asked JFK if he was going to enforce the

United States Constitution or go along with Catholic Canon Law, and Kennedy said that he would stick with the Constitution, which was signing his own death warrant. President Kennedy wanted to break up the CIA and pull out of the Vietnam War, so the godfather pope in Rome gave his blessings and approval for American mob bosses to carry out the assassination, a joint Mafia-CIA operation that involved the shooting and the subsequent cover-up. The CIA might as well be called the Catholic Intelligence Agency, since it was started by William Donovan, who used fellow Catholics as agents and operators. New Orleans mafia chieftan Carlos Marcello, Florida's head Santo Trafficante, and Chicago boss Sam Giancana helped in the planning, with the cooperation of Lyndon B. Johnson. Once he became president, Johnson catered to the Milirary-Industrial Complex, the corporations that skyrocketed in profit when Johnson expanded the Vietnam War into a decade-long bloodbath.

Vietnam, Laos, and Cambodia were parts of the colony of French Indochina until 1954, when

France lost the Battle of Dien Bien Phu to the forces of the Viet Minh. At the Geneva

Conference, the country was divided into North Vietnam, controlled by Ho Chi Minh's

communist regime, and the Republic of South Vietnam, supported and financed by the United

States. The Saigon government protected largely Catholic business interests, while trying to

promote Catholicism in a traditionally Buddhist population. Incursions and attacks by the Viet

Cong led to the establishment of sanctuary cities and genocide against Buddhists. Catholic

Canon Law states that "all those who do not bow to the pope are heretics who must be put to

death," which should be shocking to any person of faith.

The issue of killing your enemies is not Christian behavior, and God despises war. The sinful

intent of murder is made worse by the popular belief that you are snuffing out the only chance at

life for your victim. The so-called developed nations of Europe, Russia, and the Americas are

totally ignorant about reincarnation because of the Catholic church. There is no point in killing

another person because that soul will come back to life again in a form that is possibly worse

than the last one. Medical professionals must learn about reincarnation and God if they are to

council patients and family members about matter of death and dying. Doctors and lawyers are

specialists without any training in theological matters, so they live as atheists getting by on ethics

set down at the time of the Industrial Revolution. It would help a patient's morale to know that

they are just facing a transition to the next life in about sixteen months.

It is also unethical to promise people that they are going to Heaven, because no one knows who

is going to Heaven or not. The religious zealots who say that everyone goes to Heaven are

deluded and engaged in wishful thinking, for the road to Paradise is very narrow.

Morality and Sin

Humans are meant to reproduce, so men and women have been given feelings of pleasure when they copulate to ensure that children will be born so that the human race can keep going. The overemphasis on sexual pleasure usually leads to hedonism, which is the obsession with overindulgence. God wants us to have a good time, so lust is not sinful in itself, but it can cause people to ignore God totally. When people become so distracted by pleasure that they can't make time to pray twice a day, that means they are turning their backs on God while they pursue the juvenile tingling in their naughty bits. The same can be said of becoming addicted to food, drugs, alcohol, or gambling, which are activities that lead away from spirituality. Moderation should be observed in all things.

Leading others astray with false doctrine is a sin, so those who claim that Jesus is God are sinning against me by saying that I do not have my own soul. God's nature is to be jealous of any worship that is not directed towards Him. No man has seen God, and the people who claim they met Jesus in a dream or near-death experience are either imagining things or telling lies to get attention. We tend to retain our childhood need to be noticed and liked when we begin interacting with others, but in adulthood the goal changes to becoming rich and famous.

The religious fanatics on the Internet insist they are knowledgeable, so they act as the great debaters, using a prearranged series of boring platitudes to support their statements. People are led to start praying to Jesus Christ by them, although it is against the Sermon on the Mount's instructions because I cannot hear prayer or read minds. Others tell you to listen to the holy spirit, yet no voice is coming to them. Perhaps the effort is causing schizophrenia, a condition of hearing voices in your head that aren't there. Those who know don't talk, and those who talk don't know.

Misery has come to many people these days, so I hope to alleviate some of the mental anguish at least. Part of living means suffering at times, but without the duality of pain and pleasure it would be difficult to appreciate the moments of feeling happy. Most people have to endure periods of boredom, so everyone must develop the disciplines of patience, self-control, modesty, and generosity so that your soul is pure and your intentions are honest. You have to be honest to yourself before you can be honest to others.

Abortion takes away a life, so it is definitely the sin of murder. If a person does not get to live a full life span, it will take multiple future lives to catch up in terms of development of the complete soul. Since there will be no more future lifetimes, the crime of murder is worse now than ever. Awareness is only partial during life, but there will be complete memory in the afterlife. The people who are dying now might get one more reincarnation that goes into childhood and teenage years, but Judgment Day will come. The Last Day could be thirty-five years away or it could come tomorrow, so preparation is imperative. There will be no second chances after Judgment.

God despises acts of war, yet in the wars we have seen the military chaplains bless the boys going into battle and they bless the weapons that will be used to kill others. The first Christians became the Catholic church, who launched the Crusades and carried on the terror of the Inquisition. All wars since the French Revolution were engineered by the Jesuit Order of Loyola, who are sworn to kill all those who do not bow to the pope of Rome. Catholic business interests caused the Vietnam War, as well as the desire to exterminate the Buddhist population of Southeast Asia.

The Jesuit policy is to infiltrate into all departments of government and education, with their first loyalty going to the Catholic church, not their country. They include evil people such as John Kerry, James Comey, Bill and Hillary Clinton, Barack and Big Mike Obama, Anthony Fauci, Alejandro Mayorkas, and Bill Gates.

The Catholic-Zionist alliance controls the United States government and the Military Industrial Complex. President Kennedy was assassinated because he was a liberal Catholic who wanted to pull out of Vietnam and dismantle the CIA, which is exclusively Catholic. The Mafia also hated JFK because he was sharing a mistress named Judith Exner with mob bosses Sam Giancana and "Handsome Johnny" Roselli at the time when Robert Kennedy was going after the mob in his position as Attorney General. A hit team of CIA operatives caught the motorcade in a crossfire from several snipers, and they set up Lee Harvey Oswald to get arrested as the lone shooter, then a strip club owner and Mafia associate named Jack Ruby shot Oswald in the Dallas police station so he couldn't talk. Ruby and Oswald were rumored to be casually entwined in a secret homosexual cult of group sex enthusiasts.

Scripture says to call no man on this earth 'holy Father, because your only holy Father is God in Heaven. Despite Biblical instructions, millions of churchgoers address their priests as 'Father'. A priest does not represent our Creator, nor does he possess powers of bestowing blessings, transubstantiation of the flesh or forgiveness of sin. For centuries the Vatican has sent missionaries out to bring the Roman Catholic mythology and techniques of indoctrination to all populations who then start praying to multiple deities. The Hare Krishna cult is much smaller, but they also have numerous imaginary gods and statues to worship.

Populations were largely illiterate in Biblical times and throughout the Middle Ages, so stories about events had to be presented in simple terms. Calling Jesus the son of God is a poor choice of words, since it implies that was a mother involved, thus leading to the erroneous worship of Mary, who they call a divine 'mediatrix' or the immaculate mother of God. Remember that it is a sin to pray to anyone but God, yet the rosary circuit of praying consists of twenty-five Hail Mary prayers, five Lord's Prayers, and one Confiteor at the end. The Confiteor is worded in this manner:

"I confess to God and to blessed Mary ever-Virgin, to blessed Michael the Archangel and blessed John the Baptist, to the holy apostles Peter and Paul, and to blessed Leutherius and Cassian and blessed Juvenal along with all the saints and you Father:

through my fault, through my fault, my most grievous fault, I have sinned by my pride in my abundant evil iniquitous and heinous thought, speech, pollution, suggestion, delectation, consent, word and deed, in perjury, adultery, sacrilege, murder, theft, false witness, I have sinned by sight, hearing, taste, smell and touch, and in my behaviour, my evil vices. I beg blessed Virgin Mary and all the saints, and these saints and you, Father, to pray and intercede for me a sinner to our Lord Jesus Christ."

The Confiteor prayer is asking God and Mary to pray to Jesus, which is the sin of sacrilege. God has no superior, so He does not pray to anyone obviously. In the Bible, Jesus prayed to God and told everybody to do the same, yet the Catholic church insists on going against everything that is sacred. Bishop Leutherius was consecrated as the bishop of Winchester in the year 670 AD, so his name does not belong in any prayer. John Cassian was a 5th century ascetic monk who produced writings for the church and helped to set up monasteries in Egypt, while the man called Juvenal, was the Roman poet Decimus Junius Juvenalis who wrote a series of poems called the Satires, from which came the satirical form of comedy. Someone decided these influential people were saints after they died, so now they can magically read your mind when you are praying. To make matters worse, Jesus appears to be the one who is receiving and processing all the prayers from those pagan beads, which is heresy.

The mindless sheep who recite such prayers simply memorize the words and repeat them without thinking about the meaning of the content, because the teachers emphasize repetition as the effective mechanism of prayer, rather than understanding. People usually don't get specific when asking forgiveness because its easier to declare that everybody is born into sin, so they confess to other people's sins to cover all the bases.

Stealing from others is a sin when the thief takes that which does not belong to him instead of working or asking for assistance in times of need. In the city of Montreal, the young people who roam the streets have developed a subculture of stealing where they consider it normal to rob other people. Most of the citizens of Quebec province went through Catholic schools growing up, and the result has been a resentment of the church that demands their money and priest who molest their children, which in turn has led to a hatred of all religions and disbelief in God.

The Bible uses the allegory of the thief to describe the messiah coming suddenly without being seen, then to rob them of their masks of hypocrisy and ignorance. People will continue to sin and impose their phony personalities on the world, but they will be exposed.

2 Peter 3:10 " But the day of the Lord will come like a thief, and then the heavens will pass away with a roar, bodies will be burned up and dissolved, and the earth and the works that are done on it will be exposed."

Revelation 16:15 "Behold, I am coming like a thief! Blessed is the one who stays awake, keeping his garments on, that he may not go about naked and be seen exposed."

Thessalonians 5:2 "For you yourselves are fully aware that the day of the Lord will come like a thief in the night."

Televangelists steal money from gullible followers, and they will not see Heaven because they love money, not God. The carnival barkers of old have changed into religious money grubbers exploiting freedom of religion to forge a undeserved non-taxable income for themselves so that they can buy private jets and mansions. The Catholic church has always built castles amidst poverty, not appreciating the truth that it is better to give than to receive. Those who sponge wealth using religion so that can live in luxury have had their reward, and they will miss out on Heaven because they have only served themselves, not God.

God called humans self-centred, ignorant, and irresponsible. He also told me that mankind is "too stupid to remember the Ten Commandments" so I have been instructed to simplify them to three Commandments for easier comprehension:

"You shall not have any other gods before me, nor shall you offer worship to idols or icons, but love God with all your heart, your soul, and your mind."

"Do not kill."

"Do not tells lies, or steal from others, but treat your neighbor as you would like to be treated."

When people do bad things, God punishes during life as well as in the afterlife, so deeds can come back to the evildoer in a process known as Karma. It is pointless to risk retaliating against those who have harmed you, because that is God's jurisdiction.

"Never take revenge for yourselves, but leave it to the wrath of God, for it is written: "Vengeance is mine, I will repay says the Lord."

Over the years skeptics have claimed that Jesus Christ is a mythical figure who was invented by men of the past to help people feel good about themselves and to make them behave in a civilized manner. The opposite has happened. Mankind has remained uncivilized for the most part, for we live in a world where people are obsessed with killing, arguing, stealing, and lying to get what they want. When people have nothing to believe in, they have no fear of punishment in the Afterlife; they feel they can beat the odds of getting caught and repaid for their crimes. Many people scoff and deny that divine retribution will come to them. Those who think that Hell is just a fairy tale will be bitterly disappointed when they find themselves in Hell for all eternity. Only a fool believes there is no God, and they are not likely to become believers if they do not open their minds and study this book. People of faith will have this information and behave accordingly. Once you understand the truth then the truth shall make you free.

Every soul on this planet is in danger due to the relentless assaults on the truth. The authorities want to promote pagan polytheism and atheism. This is where the Vatican tactics to divide and conquer are applied. The agents of Rome's Jesuit army are dedicated to infiltration, subversion, and indoctrination. In the future, they will be able to get atheists to join Catholicism by making it mandatory, and since the atheists do not believe in God in the first place, it will not matter to them what beliefs are written down. They can live as lax Catholics like so many others who hold Baptismal certificates but do not attend church or pray.

Several religions gather people together to take part in a weekly mass led by a priest standing at an altar performing a miracle by reaching up into Heaven and bringing Christ's body and soul down to become flesh and blood to be sacrificed once again for the sins of mankind. The official dogma is that God bows His head to the priest's command, then Christ is summoned to be present in the wafers and wine. The priest is considered to be the ambassador of Christ and vice regent here on earth, with the authority of Jesus Christ to teach the gospel and to forgive repentant sinners.

Obviously, there is nobody hiding inside the magic cookie of communion, I am using my body and blood right now, thank you very much. The priests are educated men who should know better, yet they continue in their lives of superstition and lies without regard for the punishment that is coming their way.

Virtue and Righteousness

The reason we are alive is to improve our personalities and to help each other as we seek to know God. Having faith in God will lead us to do good rather than evil. Generosity is a virtue that will bring happiness to the person who is able to succeed in life well enough to help the unfortunate ones and alleviate some of the misery of this world. Greedy people who hoard money and possessions are seldom happy. Most people are raised to look down on members of society that have less material wealth, so we need to struggle against our natural tendency to show disdain towards those who are different. Tolerance is a virtue that is difficult to maintain in a neurotic world that has been divided and set against each other. Be wary of institutional charities because much of the money they collect gets siphoned off to pay their administrators lofty salaries.

James 1:27 *"Pure and undefiled religion before our God and Father is this: to care for orphans and widows in their distress and to keep oneself from being polluted by the world."*

1 John 2:15 *"Do not love the things of this world; if anyone loves the world, the love of the Father is not in them. For all that is in the material world – the desires of the flesh, the desires of the eyes, and the pride of life – they are not from the Father but from the world."*

Romans 12:2 *"Do not conform to this world but be transformed by the renewing of your mind. Then you will be able to test and approve what is the good, pleasing, and perfect will of God."*

Patience is another mental discipline that is virtuous and valuable when facing the struggles of social interaction. You must think quickly in many situations to avoid overreacting to petty arguments that get blown out of proportion when people get angry. You can win many battles but still lose the war after the dust settles down, so it's wise to think twice before acting rashly. Although it is difficult to harness a temper outburst, that lack of self-control can be conquered. Conflicts are often sparked by mere words, so the first step is to remain calm.

Patience and self-control can be developed by joining a Yoga club or learning martial arts. The techniques bring more awareness of the body and understanding of energy points known as Chakras that govern the overall health and mental state of each person. Fasting is one technique that is beneficial from time to time, since the digestion process diverts some of your consciousness to processing food, and leads away from the effort of concentration that can give you spiritual insight. Extreme fasting for more than several days is dangerous, and should not be attempted immediately, because it takes gradual practice to fast for longer periods of time, and it is difficult to start eating again after the period of fasting.

Christian fanatics denounce Yoga and meditation as witchcraft, just as they scoff at the existence of other worlds the fact that planets are spherical in shape. The flat earth movement is very outspoken in their belief that the earth is covered by a firmament and that no GPS satellites are in orbit. The zealots deny scientific measurement of the Big Bang as the start of the universe, although I have published a Physics book that explains how God caused the Big Bang of material existence using vibrations we know as sound, and the phenomenon of light to carry "the Word", which means the codes and formulas necessary for existence that pass through my soul. God works through me, but He exists in everyone and in every molecule of matter. Physicists Max Planck, Einstein, and Werner Heisenberg could not come forward and say they believed in God for fear of ridicule by atheist scientists, but they knew deep down that God is the matrix of all matter and consciousness.

The falsehood of the trinity causes intelligent people to leave religion completely, and drives others into insanity when they cannot resolve the puzzle of three gods being the same as one. The mental gymnastics required to accept Trinitarianism as reality leads to a breakdown of the subconscious and violent behavior filled with resentment. Those who profess Christianity are the creepiest people in society, always ready to denounce Muslims and insult the name of Allah as they declare themselves saved. Fanatical Christians will turn down the chance to go to Heaven and stay with the false triune gods right up until the end, and they will reject the truth that Jesus and Muhammad are the same man, and Allah is the real God Yahweh, not the fictional deities of the trinity. Ministers are trained to argue against any doctrine that conflicts with theirs.

The effort to get rid of God is expressed in the New Age Universalist concept, where speakers like David Icke are teaching that we are part of one gigantic communal soul governing the laws of nature ourselves unconsciously without a Creator. The human ego is out of control, so people are attracted to groups who promote the idea that mankind is the highest form of life in the universe. A vast majority of people do not believe in God or planets with different civilizations in various stages of advancement and decline. God told me that the human race is around the middle in terms of scientific development, and that there are over ten thousand more advanced civilizations in the Milky Way Galaxy alone, so the universe is teeming with life. He did not mention anything about space travel however, so that remains an open question.

Outspoken religious people are overly concerned with minute details that they hope will prop up their beliefs. They always seem to be arrogant overbearing pedants who feel compelled to criticize anything that is said to them, citing the Bible as an infallible source of wisdom. In fact there are many problems with the Bible due to the words passing through different scribes, oral tradition, and translation through various languages. The Old Testament was written in mostly in the Hebrew language, with the prophecies in Ezra, Daniel, and one verse in Jeremiah written in Aramaic.

The New Testament was written from 50 to 100 AD in Greek, which was the scholastic language at that time. Between 200 BC and 300 BC, the Jewish elders did a Greek translation of the Old Testament, called the Septuagint, that became widely accepted and was even used in many synagogues. The Book of Exodus states that male and female slaves are the property of their owner, who is allowed to beat them whenever he wants as long as the slave does not die, in which case the slave owner should be punished. Physical slavery was never resolved in the New Testament, which only speaks of spiritual slavery, so owning slaves is technically still legal and slave owners can beat their slaves, which is obviously abhorrent to God.

Spiritual slavery is in place through the lies and propaganda of the television networks and newspapers owned by the wealthy elite who wish to enslave all of mankind physically through a gradual erosion of civil rights put into place while the population is busy enjoying bread and circuses while they are secretly being robbed. The moon landings turned out to look so easy that the public became bored after repeated broadcasts that tanked in the ratings and were discontinued. They diverted attention away from the black starless background by planting flags, showing a footprint, hitting golf balls, and scooting around on the moon buggies.

The earth is surrounded by the two Van Allen Radiation Belts and one new layer of radiation caused by the USA exploding a nuclear weapon in that area in an attempt to penetrate that barrier to space travel. The experiment was unsuccessful however, and just made the situation worse. Since President Kennedy promised to land a man on the moon before the decade was finished, the government produced a movie simulation and televised it as a monumental event in history. History is largely a string of lies told by those who are in charge.

Any human would have to be protected by six feet of lead to survive a journey through the Van Allen belts, and the weight of the shielding would be too much for the Saturn Five rocket's limited propulsion. NASA was started using the knowledge of Nazi scientists that were brought to the USA in Operation Paperclip, the most notable being Werner Von Braun, who developed the V1 and V2 vengeance weapons using slave labor. All war crimes were forgiven for these monsters by the American government.

The CIA was founded by Catholic William Donovan and it is funded by the American taxpayers, but their first allegiance is to the pope, and drumming up money to carry out the wishes of the Vatican.

The Jesuits hold major positions of power in the USA, and we see this in the border disaster of illegal immigrants being allowed to cross in the millions. South and Central American countries are exclusively Catholic from the days of the Spaniards, so the newcomers are expected to vote for the Democrat Party controlled by the Jesuits.

Professional politicians like Joe Biden and Barack Obama are planted to carry out the policy of the Vatican on orders from billionaire George Soros, who controls Obama, Biden, and that ridiculously stupid Vice-President Kamala Harris. The time of this writing is the year 2024, so I hope these insidious puppets will be replaced. Joe Biden has never had a real job or done any military service. In 2023, Joe Biden announced that they planned to go back to the moon in a joint Canada-USA program. Prime Minister Justin Trudeau was also raised in Catholic schools, and both men are atheists. Biden cannot even bring himself to say the word 'God' in his speeches. The Epstein Island list includes Trudeau, Hunter Biden, and Joe Biden. It is embarrassing and dangerous to have such creepy people in power, for they want another world war. Tensions have already boiled over in Palestine, Syria, Iran, and Ukraine so they may get their World War Three if anyone flinches.

There are numerous Catholic celebrities who are on the pedophile list as frequent visitors to the island, both males and females who are active Catholics or connected to the church financially. Actor Tom Hanks was a raised as a Catholic, then his mother became a Mormon, and he states that he is now a Bible-toting evangelical Christian. Hanks is also well-known as a pedophile obsessed with little girls. The Epstein Island list also include devout Catholic television host Stephen Colbert, pop star Madonna, Robert DeNiro, and Catholic-Jewish atheist loudmouth Whoopie Goldberg, whose real name is Caryn Elaine Johnson. These people have given up eternity in Heaven to indulge themselves in perverse fornication, so they will be tormented in Hell forever for their gluttonous sexual behavior and substance abuse.

Vatican City is a very rich independent state with collection of real estate properties around the world and they possess a vast store of valuable artifacts, documents, and art accumulated over many centuries. In recent years, the Holy See has spent millions to settle child molestation cases and legal fees to protect their priests from criminal prosecution.

There are many wealthy people who have descended into perversion and who have gone to the island on numerous occasions, such as King Phillip of the UK, Prince Andrew, Barack Obama, Michelle Obama, Bill Clinton, and Hillary Clinton. They consider themselves to be royalty, so they use children like toys that can be used and discarded according to their whims. Not only Catholic priests have been arrested around the world for child molestation, the Southern Baptist organization has a major problem with thousands of their ministers being caught exploiting children sexually. All citizens should do what they can to call out those who harm children and expose them for what they are.

There are numerous cults around the world led by Jesus imposters. A.J. Miller runs a compound in Australia, claiming he is the reincarnation of Jesus Christ, and that his girlfriend is Mary Magdelene. Miller was kicked out of the Jehovah's Witnesses, so he has establish the Divine Truth Mission in Queensland. In Russia, an ex-traffic cop named himself Vissarion and started a cult with millions of followers. He operated for over twenty years but was arrested and jailed in 2017 when the authorities shut down his ministry.

The third fake Jesus is Apollo Quiboloy in the Philippines, still operating and collecting vast amounts of money from a population that earns an average of two dollars a day. These men have no fear of God, and they will pay for their lies in the Afterlife, alone in disgrace except for invisible tormentors reminding them that they will suffer for all eternity for their insolence and for leading others astray.

Any new idea that presents an inconvenient truth goes through three stages: first it is mocked and ridiculed, then there is a violent reaction to oppose it, and finally the truth is accepted as self-evident, and others will try to take credit for it. The individuals who have insulted me will not be forgiven because there is hatred on their lips and violence in their hearts. There is no indication that evil souls will ever change their minds, see the light, and offer apologies to me.

I have contacted many churches about my existence, but they have all rejected me as the return of Jesus, calling me various names and rebuking me as hard as they can. The little power trippers rule over their various congregations of blind sheep, and they are secure in their domains. They are not curious to learn new things, and they have lost all fear of God's wrath. As the Bible says, "Fear no man, but fear only God." Since I am anointed to carry out God's will, people should respect and obey me instead of worshipping my image from what they hear from preachers or what they see in the movies.

There are numerous sects using the word Christianity. According to Gordon-Conwell Theological Seminary, there are roughly forty-three thousand Christian denominations worldwide in 2012. That is up from five hundred in 1800 and thirty-nine thousand in 2008, but this number is expected to grow to fifty-five thousand by the year 2025. They have different beliefs, and everybody can't be right. The world has Roman Catholic, Eastern Orthodox, Mormon, Jehovah's Witness, Seventh Day Adventist, Baptist, Lutheran, Methodist, Presbyterian, Christian Science, United Church, Amish, Quaker, Mennonite, Anglican, Episcopal, Oriental Orthodox, Church of Christ, Foursquare Church, Divine Truth Mission, and many more.

Ardent Catholic producer Mel Gibson released a truly mythical movie called "The Passion of the Christ", which made me cringe, for it depicts me as a greasy bearded coward having a nervous breakdown during the Crucifixion and crying in pain. I am quite familiar with pain, and I do not cry out or lift my voice in agony. In the television series, they portray me as an ugly longhair with a strange accent quoting passages from the New Testament that were not written until centuries later, mostly from hearsay and the opinions of the writers. Exploiting people's emotions using the Jesus brand name has made millions for many people, but their gold and silver will not help them on Judgment Day when I will say, "I never knew you, depart from me into the eternal fire my Father has prepared for Satan and his angels to torment you forever." The souls who are sent to Hell will exist in an environment tailored to their worst fears and insecurities where they will hear voices reminding them of their next upcoming torture, day after day, and humiliating them for their failings in their callous disregard for the lives they have ruined. "*They will be sorry they ever got born*", says the Lord.

When contemplating the great beyond, logical people might think the afterlife is possible, but they hate the thought of being in stuck in Heaven with all those tedious religious fanatics they see on television and shouting from street corners. They would rather be with their friends in Hell, where at least they will know somebody. Two things are wrong with those assumptions, because the zealots and preachers are not the ones who will make it to Heaven, and it is likely that the souls in Hell will not be able to communicate with each other at all. The awareness of being locked in Hades forever will be worse than anyone can imagine, just as the intense pleasure of Heaven cannot be appreciated until you get there. Each soul will have a Heavenly body that experiences continuous rushes in many places, and you will be in control of summoning up past memories from any of your previous lives at will simultaneously.

The meaning of "the day of the Lord" in the Bible refers to Judgment Day, not my birth as a man to do the chores assigned to me as the messiah of humanity. As it is written, "*the day of the Lord will come like a thief in the night, then the world will be burned up and be dissolved with a roar*". The works of the wicked will be exposed as the living and those in the Interitum will evaporate and rise to be Judged.

The evil enemies of truth will be separated from the good, and I will lock the Gates of Heaven and Hell forever. So listen and be wise so that you do not fall into deception and miss out on eternal Paradise.

Learning ancient Chinese physical disciplines gave me insight and spiritual awareness along with greater control of my bodily processes. It is difficult to achieve complete muscle relaxation and the stillness necessary for soul travelling. One of the reasons for writing this book is to inform people that God says "the Bible has some problems", without elaborating further. This forced me to examine the verses, where I see that there are contradictions and wording that can be misinterpreted. Instead of debating things endlessly, priority should be placed on knowing the essentials of how to get your own personal soul in a pure enough state to qualify for Heaven. Do not assume you will be saved by participating in a revival gathering raising your hands to the sky shouting "hallelujah", because that only provides an adrenaline thrill for a short time. The preachers know how mass psychology works to get a crowd going.

When the joy of the church meeting wears off, the congregation is anxious to repeat the event, so the whole experience becomes rather addictive. People are sociable, so it would not be enjoyable to pray alone at home in private. Small town people might know most of the people they see at church, so it would be unthinkable to wander off and change to another denomination. My suggestion is that all believers make sure their preachers are following this book and learning to speak the truth about reincarnation caused by one God, not a trinity of false gods. Anyone who contradicts me will be refused entry to Heaven on Judgment Day.

Reincarnation is easy to see manifested in population statistics, where the world's population quadrupled in the twentieth century, from two billion to nearly eight billion, despite the billions of deaths caused by the two world wars, Korea, Vietnam, and Afghanistan. The notion of people having one life only makes killing all that more sinful, since the murderer's intention is to take away the one chance of living from his victim. Most writings of people who cling to their religion of Catholicism express distaste for the pope and the many child molesters of the priesthood, but they still defend Catholicism. The church claims to be universal, so they can't have it both ways.

Race and gender are no barriers to reincarnation, so it is important to use that fact when teaching tolerance of others in schools. We have all lived lives as both male and female in six basic racial groups, so we should strive to treat everybody as equals. There are traits of famous females of history that are highly unusual in their effect on the social order, such as Joan of Arc and Queen Elizabeth I of England. Those were famous females who stood out as outstanding during their lives and legendary in their notoriety, so it is possible they were the same soul.

To review a simple teaching, the Sermon on the Mount tells you how to pray. When you pray, you must not be like the hypocrites who love to stand and pray in the synagogues and at the street corners, that they may be seen by others. Truly, I say to you, they have received their reward. But when you pray, go into your room and shut the door and pray to your Father who is in secret. And your Father who sees in secret will reward you. And when you pray, do not chant or heap up empty phrases as the pagans do, for they think that they will be heard for their many words. Do not be like them, for your Father knows what you need before you ask him.

There seems to be evidence that bad things happen to people and countries that hold the wrong religious beliefs. For example, Colonel Claus von Stauffenberg was a staunch Catholic who volunteered to plant a briefcase bomb under a table next to Hitler in 1944, which would enable a coup d'etat to begin against the Third Reich. The bomb exploded, but failed to kill the dictator due to the thickness of the wooden table leg where the briefcase was relocated by another officer after Stauffenberg left the room. He was captured and shot by a firing squad shortly thereafter, and the plot to take over the government failed. Hitler was raised as a Catholic, but after coming to power, he became his own religion and started persecuting the church and anyone else who dared to disagree with his policies. Stauffenberg had told a priest all about the plot earlier in confession, which was very risky in those days of totalitarianism. There is no indication that the priest informed on him, but if the investigation had gone on longer, the Gestapo might have paid the priest a visit to obtain some names using their well-known torture techniques.

Hitler attributed his lucky escapes to "providence", since he cast belief in God aside and decided he was Germany's messiah, leading to his bitter end in the Berlin bunker. The war started with Poland's destruction, and it was mainly Catholic, with many Jewish residents. The Nazi inner circle consisted of men who were raised Catholic, so it seems obvious that there is something wrong with those religions, since God wasn't protecting any of them.

The Japanese suffered destruction because they worshipped Emperor Hirohito as their living god, which of course infuriated the real God even more than the three false gods of Christianity. The atheistic USSR lost millions of people in the war, and of course the national background was Orthodox Christian Trinitarian before communism took over. Those Russians who worshipped in secret also hailed Mary like the Roman Catholics.

The empty words from the voices of evangelists wail out to those with ears that are hungry for reassurance, as they are controlled by the images and idols that rule the world. Hollywood has exploited the greasy bearded long haired Jesus icon in numerous movies to make the public believe that all their past, present, and future sins are automatically forgiven because God came down one time only to be a victim of a blood sacrifice for universal redemption. The result of this brainwashing is seen in the hostile, gluttonous, and perverted behavior of Christian preachers, priests, celebrities, and corrupt government officials.

The Four Noble Truths

Life is a journey, so we must know our destination in order to find the correct path. Any new idea that presents an inconvenient truth goes through three stages: first it is mocked and ridiculed, then there is a violent reaction, and finally the truth is accepted as self-evident, and others will try to take credit for it. Your personal path has twists and turns along the way that can guide you to wisdom or lead you astray, but when you know the truth you can reach your predestined place. The factor of free will allows people to turn their backs on God, which puts those who ignore their Creator into another destiny than the one God has offered them.

Buddhism and Christianity arose independently of each other, separated as they were by almost three thousand miles and five hundred years. The principle texts of both Buddhism and Christianity were written down only after decades, and in some cases centuries, had passed since the founder's death, leaving plenty of time to organize oral tradition into familiar and acceptable frameworks. Buddha lived in a society of atheists, while Jesus lived in a very religious environment where people already accepted God. Buddha took great care to explain he was not a deity, as did Jesus, who said in the Book of John: "I can do nothing on my own. I judge as God tells me. Despite the words of the Bible, people still insist on wrongly preaching that Jesus is God in the flesh who only came to mankind on one occasion.

Although reincarnation is discussed in Buddhism and Hinduism, there are outdated notions of how the rebirth cycle works. They teach that a soul can reincarnate in the animal kingdom, as another human, or as a spirit. The truth is that human beings always reincarnate as new human beings, and we have no control over the process. No one is looking for the reincarnation of Buddha because the writings say that Gautama Buddha did not wish to come back.

The Sanskrit word 'dukkha' encompasses suffering, painful experiences, and things that cannot be satisfied. The First Noble Truth is that these are innate characteristics of Samsara, the worldly life and rebirth cycle.

The Second Noble Truth is 'samudaya', which refers to the cause of suffering. The concept is called 'tanha', which means 'craving'. This includes attachment to pleasures of the senses, trying to be somebody you are not, and the desire to stop something from happening instead of accepting it.

The Third Noble Truth is 'nirodha' - the ending of suffering. This is attained by renouncement or letting go of the material world.

'Magga', the Fourth Noble Truth is the Eightfold Path of right view, right resolve, right speech, right conduct, right livelihood, right effort, mindfulness, and meditative union.

The things of this world are temporary, so it is useless to become attached to material goods or to wallow in the pleasures of the flesh. Spartan lifestyles are admirable, but they might be too far from the 'happy medium' experience, or the 'middle way'. Self-denial comes through logic, so life should not be completely devoid of pleasure.

We are taught from birth to obtain popularity, to pursue money, and to desire luxury; this creates the fear of losing those things. There is no fear for one whose mind is not filled with desires. Attachment is the cause of suffering, so we can be genuinely happy once we overcome these desires and learn the meaning of life. The measure of a successful soul is not determined by the property that the person owned during their lifetime.

Many wealthy people have stated that they are not happy at all. An ideal society would be one in which all citizens could live comfortably without excess wealth or extreme poverty.

Therefore, my judgment is just, because I carry out the will of the one who sent me, not my own will. And the Father who sent me, He has testified of me. You have neither heard His voice at any time nor seen His form." Unfortunately, modern Christians ignore those passages, and insist that Jesus claimed he was one with the Father, without including the rest of the verse that says all people are connected to God. "I do not pray for these alone, but also for those who will believe in me through their word; that they all may be one, as you, Father, are in me, and I in you; that they also may be one in us, that the world may believe that you sent me. The glory which you gave me I have given them, that they may be one just as we are one: I in them, and you in me; that they may be made perfect in one, and that the world may know that you have sent me, and have loved them as you have loved me." Humans have changed the meaning of the verse to suit their ongoing pagan desire to have a physical God that they can see, so that they can make statues to worship.

Buddha once said, "The faults of others are easier to see than one's own." Five centuries later, Jesus uttered these words: "Why do you see the splinter in someone else's eye and never notice the log in your own?" People are quick to judge others as evil and sinful.

Life is a learning process and there will be a test when it is over. Only those people who strive for wisdom can meet each challenge and be satisfied that they have achieved something worthwhile. The stakes in this sublimely tedious game of existence are very high, since it involves the destination of your eternal soul. When we visualize the concept of being conscious forever as the total soul there is no grey area available, so reward or punishment will be the ultimate state of your existence for all eternity. That leaves people no choice but to strive for Heaven; those who do not care about suffering in Hell will likely end up there. God will not accept those who are sceptical of Him. People think that Hell will be a giant gathering of rebellious people having a wild party together when it will actually be a desperate lonely confinement. The non-believers are foolish, because they have wagered everything on nothing.

It is essential that any useful religious doctrine be based on the concept of eternal reward or punishment and the existence of God. The religion of Jainism has no God, so it must be labelled as an atheist cult rather a proper religion. The Jains believe that matter created life and that matter had no beginning, despite the measurement of the Big Bang by science and Einstein's formula that shows that matter is energy. Matter is a wave that must be observed by a consciousness to collapse into particle form that can be experienced as solid forms. The human race and all other life forms were designed by God, despite the egotistical scientists who teach that we are so clever that we climbed out of a pool of chemicals and worked our way up through the animal kingdom. DNA is a highly complex code, and codes require a programmer.

These words are meant to be for those who care about achieving eternal reward, so I offer teachings, not preachings. I will not beg for sinners to repent, for they will never change from their egotistical path of contempt for all information that conflicts with their existing beliefs. My aim is not to deal with people's sins, but to save those who are eager to learn the truth about what is necessary to attain Heaven on Judgment Day. Everything is at stake in the game of life, yet most people do not care about their ultimate fate in the afterlife, acting as if purifying their intentions is a trivial matter in salvation.

Some misguided religions teach that everyone will go to Heaven, no matter what they have done on this earth. That kind of wishful thinking defies all logic, and it clearly contradicts what is written in scripture about Heaven and Hell.

Philosophers post their ideas on social media or lurk in coffee shops to proclaim opinions from minds that are locked shut. They will not accept any facts except for those ideas that agree with their beliefs. Religions are densely populated with closed-minded souls clinging to rigid story lines. Groups recite stale phrases without deep meaning, only mysterious words of a vague redemption from sin or proclamations of sacrifice or repentance. Platitudes are poor substitutes for logical statements. Mankind's trend has always been to degenerate back to mythology and idol worship in the vain hope that some of the gods they have invented will help them.

Each person should focus on bringing his or her soul back to equilibrium during and after all experiences. It takes a conscious effort to get the entire body and mind to relax, so it helps to join a Tai Chi club or learn breathing techniques that can be done even from a sitting position. There is a system known as Chi Kung (also spelled 'Qi Gong') that accomplishes the task of health through relaxation. Yoga and martial arts include breathing exercises that help to strengthen the inner energy.

Life becomes more tolerable when we get a grip on ourselves enough to avoid flying off into anger. Self-control helps a person to stay on a firm path in life by reducing impulsive behavior. Decision making takes a certain relaxed confidence, so a person will make fewer mistakes by staying in control of the emotions and thinking clearly. There are days when you might be treated rudely by three or four people, so the anger creeps up and you will feel a distaste for the next person you meet before they say anything. If we stay aware of human frailty in social encounters, we can recover from each rejection faster. It is a pipe dream that all people will accept us unconditionally so we can anticipate some abuse and keep our thoughts on more important matters than trying to impress strangers.

Purity of intention is all-important to qualify for the eternal reward. Each person is on a journey, so there must be a destination. Those souls who are righteous and faithful to God will be allowed into Heaven. The fear of God is the hatred of evil, so those who do not fear God do not hate evil. Most souls will not be prepared, and so they will be locked in the Underworld forever. Whether you call it Hell or Hades, it is the same destination – an eternal and painful environment tailor-made to a person's worst fears.

People usually live in a state of denial concerning unpleasant matters, so most humans do not care about Hell. Many refuse to believe that they will be punished for their disbelief and their crimes against others. Evil people mock God to amuse others and to divert attention away from their crooked personalities. If people knew the Fourfold Path, they would realize that they are attacking themselves when they abuse others. No one can injure God; efforts to insult your Creator are suicidal. The only thing that matters in life is achieving Heaven on the Last Day.

My advice is to pray twice a day at least, and keep a life long special request prayer going throughout the years. A person can improve the purity of the soul by trying to understand those events that cause grief, for all things shall pass. We each go through unpleasant moments that seem disastrous to the point where we feel there is no use in going on. With strong faith there is hope for a wonderful future, for you can win God's approval by expressing thanks to Him in prayer. If you have God on your side nothing can harm you....no fear will block your joyful awareness for all eternity. The events of all previous lives will be available for you to relive at your will once your soul is placed into the Heavenly state. Those who deny God will experience nothing but fear and punishment in the lonely and humiliating depths of Satan's realm.

The Dead Sea Scrolls prophecy describing me was translated and verified by the Dominican Order who operate Notre Dame University, but the verse is never discussed since religious leaders are not too thrilled about the thought of Jesus coming to upstage them. There is no reason that such wording would be written down in that age unless it was a genuine prophesy from God, so it will surely come to pass that my rule over the living will be great, which is reassuring. With some prominent officials on my side, there is a chance I can prevent further misery in the world. The armed forces leaders must sit down with the political leaders and confer with me.

There must be a movement to get rid of the pedophiles in government and the clergy, as well as stopping war and slavery by supporting my actions when I come into the public eye officially. The media has ignored all of my emails because the disbelieving bosses would fire anybody who announced that the messiah has arrived. The perverts, atheists and religious fanatics are not likely to change their ways, so the wise ones who accept the truth will be the ones who will be saved from eternal damnation. It is hard to accept the fact that the human race has had the proverbial biscuit as far as the physical world is concerned, and all souls are going to the afterlife to be either rewarded or punished. The events leading up to the Last Day will be most unpleasant, but those who are faithful need not worry, for Heaven is around the corner.

Descendants of the Rothschild aristocracy are controlling the levers of power behind the curtains. Catholics and Freemasons are tools of the Zionists. The double headed eagle of the Rothschild family is the same as the 33rd Scottish Rite of Freemasonry. Asmodeus, the king of demons in Jewish legend, is coming for them. The pope wears a yarmulke because he's responsible to the Talmudic Jewish elites. Satan truly is the god of this world, working through the secret societies of wealthy bankers, tycoons, and politicians with fancy law degrees who know how to exploit the paperwork of government to their advantage. The Catholic religion is total heresy, as is Talmudic Judaism, which speaks of Jesus being in Hell swimming in the devil's semen. False beliefs are murderous, because it is much more damaging to destroy the person's soul forever than to kill the body. You can't kill the soul, and the real definition of death is to be alive in Hell for eternity. In the Bible, ending up in Hades is called the second death.

Children are innocent, so they follow along with whatever the adults are doing. In a Catholic upbringing, a student assumes that clutching a crucifix and rosary beads gives your prayers extra zing, when those objects are mere idols which is a sin against the Second

Commandment. In the Middle Ages, using idols and talking to saints became increasingly popular, but the church has not progressed in knowledge one iota here in modern times. If the pope had any sense of reality, he would turn the Vatican over to me so that I can teach the truth that will give people a chance to save themselves. The priests and bishops are set in their ways and happy with the status quo, so they cannot afford to have Jesus hanging around and they will simply deny my existence. Certain people will try to plot against me, but all their designs will fail. They cannot kill me, because I will keep coming back until God is satisfied that I have reaped enough souls to populate Heaven sufficiently. Acts 17:24 *"The God who made the world and everything in it is the Lord of Heaven and earth and does not live in temples built by human hands. He is not served by human hands, as if He needed anything. Rather, He himself gives life, breath, and everything else. From one man He made all nations that they should inhabit the whole earth; He marked out their appointed times in history and the boundaries of their lands. God did this so they would seek Him and perhaps reach out for Him and find Him, though He is not far from any one of us. In God we live and move and have our being."*

The Poisoning of Populations

Society today is full of spiritual pollution, as well as psychological and physical poisons. Politicians and private corporate interests exert control over populations, and they are striving for ever more power to intrude into people's lives. The ultimate goal is to forge a society of masters and slaves.

James 1:27 *"Pure and undefiled religion before our God and Father is this: to care for orphans and widows in their distress and to keep oneself from being polluted by the world."*

There were protests in many countries against totalitarian mandates, but in Canada those who took part in the truckers convoy protest in Ottawa had their bank accounts frozen and their credit cards cancelled, so they suddenly became non-citizens without freedom.

Justin Trudeau's minority government (propped up by the support of Jagmeet Singh's NDP party) invoked the Emergencies Act, which suspends the Canadian Charter of Rights and Freedoms. Most counties coerced people into taking a series of vaccinations, which is a war crime under the Nuremberg Codes. If people did not take the jabs, they lost their jobs.

The day was March 5, 2020, when a general lockdown was put into place, supposedly for three weeks in Ontario...it did not end after three weeks, the lockdown was in place for over two years, causing a large number of small businesses to close forever. There was no live music, no entry to buildings without a mask, mandatory testing up the nose with a long stick in places like dentist's offices. The plot is global, and very sneaky. The World Economic Forum is part of the New World Order assault of mankind and national sovereignty. The secret societies want a population of obedient zombies.

If the virus was passing through the air in crowds or spread when shaking hands or by touching money, the whole world would have died quickly. Viruses are created from within your cells; toxins come from outside the body. Illness arises as a result of systemic toxicity, not because the body has been invaded by an irresistible pathogen nearby. Part of the immune response is to create viruses to clean up poisons. Viruses dissolve toxic matter when body tissue is too toxic for living bacteria or microbes to feed upon without being poisoned to death. Without viruses, the human body could not achieve homeostasis and sustain itself in the face of systemic toxicity. Viruses are specific; they dissolve specific tissues in the body. They do this with the assistance of antibodies. Viruses are discriminatory by nature, made by the body for a specific purpose. They are not indiscriminate killers.

Viruses are exosomes - solvents for toxic cells. The more toxicity you have in your body, the more viral activity you will have. The only vector transmission of a virus is through blood transfusion or vaccines. Viruses cannot infect you by jumping from one body to another. In addition to aborted human fetus tissue, the vaccine industry relies on DNA from species such as birds, dogs, monkeys, cows, pigs, mice, and insects in vaccine manufacturing. Other deadly ingredients are mercury, liquid aluminum, formaldehyde, nickel, and chemicals used as antifreeze for cars. The human immune system is more than capable of dealing with illness when the person is healthy and not full of toxins. The entire Covid-19 scare is based on superstition, not science. I refer to Antoine Bechamp's belief that "an organism's macerozymes are unique to it and are not interchangeable with those of another". Bechamp would certainly disapprove of introducing the macerozymes of one species into an animal of another species, which is exactly what vaccines do. It is especially foolhardy when the macerozymes are already morbidly transformed and are accompanied by preservatives, formaldehyde, antifreeze, mercury, and other deadly toxins.

Tiffany Dover was a nurse at a Catholic hospital who took her injection live on television, then collapsed to the floor nineteen minutes later. She died later that evening, but the media hid her death; the newscasters went to great lengths to pretend that Tiffany was still alive until the whole episode was eventually forgotten by the fickle public.

Brainwashing is listed as a war crime, yet it is being done around the world through a fear campaign, using the media to bombard the public with hysterical messages of a rapidly mutating invisible monster roving the land in search of victims. In the '60s the KGB did experiments with that form of brainwashing. They found that after two months of feeding the subjects fear messages verbally, they could not change their minds even when confronted with true facts later.

The tribulations that many people are experiencing as we enter the year 2023 started a century ago, when the monolithic conspiracy that seeks to enslave mankind obtained financial power (and thus political power) with the introduction of the Federal Reserve banking system in 2013. A year earlier, the millionaires who were opposed to central banking were lured aboard the maiden voyage of the ocean vessel Titanic so that they would perish in the sinking. Titanic's captain Smith was a Jesuit agent who was so indoctrinated that he gave his life as well, going full speed into an iceberg field. In those days there were many spotter boats that patrolled the shipping lanes in order to give warnings via telegraph about icebergs ahead, but the warnings were ignored. The millionaire bankers who planned the scheme cancelled their suites just before heading out into the Atlantic Ocean. The pandemic scare is also the work of the Jesuit Army of the Vatican. The new fake crisis is the climate "emergency" that is being advertised on the legacy media, another arm of the New World Order.

It is troubling to know that the unelected rich people who proclaim themselves leaders are out to exterminate populations for the sake of the environment. The leader of this corporate fascism is Klaus Schwab, whose father was a prominent Nazi during the short reign of Adolf Hitler. Climate agitator John Kerry came from a wealthy family who made their fortune in the China Trade, the business selling opium to victimized people who became addicts. John Kerry is a Jesuit coadjutor doing the dirty work for the pope.

The Rockefeller family controls the wealth and the politics of the USA to this day. They work behind the scenes through their agents such as the Bush family, who have become the royal family of America. The Bushes and Rockefellers were German nobility historically tied to the Holy Roman Empire. The European controllers are the Rothschild family members who run the Central Banks and act as the Vatican bankers.

The intentions of the wealthy elite are expressed in a declaration known as the Rockefeller Masonic Creed, explaining how they have been poisoning the masses. Like Bill Gates, the Rockefellers are eugenicists, they believe they should cull the herd by shortening their lives and controlling all aspects of life. This is how the plot reads:

"We will keep their lives short and their minds weak while pretending to do the opposite. We will use our knowledge of science and technology in subtle ways so that they never know what is happening. We will use soft metals, aging accelerators, and sedatives in food and water as well as in the air. They will be covered in poisons wherever they turn. The soft metals will make them lose their minds. We will promise to find a cure from our many funds, and yet we will give them more poison. Chemical poisons will be absorbed through the skin of idiots who believe that certain hygiene products presented by great actors and musicians will bring eternal youth to their faces and bodies; through their thirsty and hungry mouths we will destroy their minds and systems of internal organs. Their children will be born disabled and deformed, and we will hide this information. The poisons will be hidden in everything around them, in what they drink, eat, breathe, and wear. We have to be ingenious in distributing the poisons because the people can see far. We will teach them that poisons are good with funny pictures and musical tones on TV. Those who are looking for them are helpful. We will enroll them to push our poisons. They will see that our products are used in films; they will get used to them and will never know the true effect. When they give birth, we will inject poisons into the blood of their children and convince them that we are helping them! We will start earlier, when their minds are young, we will target their children with what children love the most – sweet things. When their teeth decay, we will fill them with soft metals that will kill their minds and steal their future. When their ability to learn has been affected, we have created drugs that will make them sicker and cause them other illnesses, for which we will create more drugs. We will make them docile and weak before us by our power. They will grow depressed, slow and obese, and when they come to ask us for help, we will give them more poison. We will focus attention on money and material goods so that they never connect with their inner selves. We will distract them with fornication, external pleasures, and video games, so they are never one with the unity of all. Their minds will belong to us, and they will do as we say. If they refuse,

we will find ways to implement technology that alters the mind in their lives. We will use fear as our weapon. We will establish governments and establish opposition within them. We will own both sides. We will always hide our goal, but we will continue our plan. They will do the work for us, and we will prosper from their toil."

"Our families will never mix with theirs. Our blood must be pure (because it is). We will make them kill each other when they oppose us. We will keep them separate from unity through dogma and religion. We will control all aspects of their lives and tell them what to think, and how. We will guide them kindly and let them believe that they are guiding themselves. We will instigate animosity among them through our factions. When a light shines among them, we will extinguish it by mockery or death, which suits us best. We will make them tear their hearts apart and kill their own children. We will accomplish this using hatred as our ally, anger as our friend. Hatred will completely blind them, and they will never see that in their conflicts we will be their leaders. They will be busy killing each other. They will bathe in their own blood and kill their neighbors, as long as we see that they are against us. We will benefit greatly from this, for they will not see us, for they cannot see us. We will continue to prosper from their wars and their deaths. We will repeat this until our ultimate goal is achieved. We will continue to make them live in fear and anger; we will give them images and sounds. We will use all the tools we have to achieve this. The tools will be provided by their work. We will make them hate themselves and their neighbors. We will take over their lands, resources, and wealth to exercise control over them. We will trick them into accepting laws that will steal the little freedom that they have. We will set up a money system that will shut them down forever, keeping them and their children in debt. When we ban them altogether, we will accuse them of murder and present a different story to the world because we own all the media. We will use the media to control the flow of information and their feelings in our favor. When they rise up against us,

*we will crush them like insects, because they are less than that. They will
be helpless to do anything about it."*

The 2020 world pandemic hoax has shown the vast control wielded
by the corrupt government health agencies who profit from the misery
of the people. The New World Order conspirators have spent decades
conditioning the public to line up for influenza vaccines regularly, and
people have cooperated without asking why a doctor's prescription is
not needed. When the new series of shots was forced on the world,
the issue of confidentiality of medical records was stricken down by
mandates. The results of the mRNA needles have been disastrous, yet
no official has suffered punishment for the murder and crippling of
hundreds of thousands of victims. They just keep bringing out one
booster shot after the other, forcing the poison into children by law.
Some doctors say that constant boosters will cause the immune system
to fail completely.

The pandemic panic being sold to the public as a "medical
emergency" is really a method of human control and oppression. The
Center for Disease Control uses propaganda to bring in a totalitarian
state which overrides all personal rights, claiming to be the answer to
the very problem they created. The CDC owns the patents on the
disease and the dozens of vaccines pretending to cure it. The Chinese
biological laboratory in Wuhan is owned by GlaxoSmithKline, which
owns Pfizer.

Funding for the gain-of-function research at the Wuhan lab was
arranged by Anthony Fauci, who promotes the vaccines.
GlaxoSmithKline is managed by the finance company Blackrock,
which manages the finances of George Soros' Open Foundation
Company. Soros owns the German company Winterthur, which built
the Chinese laboratory in Wuhan and was bought by the German
Allianz, which has Vanguard as a shareholder. Vanguard in turn is a
shareholder of Blackrock, which controls central banks and manages

about one third of all global investment capital. Blackrock is also a major shareholder of Microsoft, owned by Bill Gates.

The World Health Organization is facilitating a global health dictatorship, commanding all member nations to enforce lockdowns and far-reaching medical edicts that empower government authorities and the vaccine industry. The constant booster shots destroy the human immune system, so the recipients may experience neural degeneration as they age, resulting in Multiple Sclerosis or rare cancers. The idea is to weaken the population so that most will need intense medical attention; the masses will be too busy surviving to resist the fascist takeover. The dictatorship aims to give rise to a medical apartheid, which will be a system of segregation that punishes healthy people for not complying.

The World Economic Forum has declared that God is dead, and that they have the ability to create life. The elites claim to be intelligent, yet they do not realize that they will be sent to Hell's lowest layer. The statement that God is dead comes from philosopher Friedrich Nietzsche of course, so Klaus Schwab is parroting a tired mantra concerning the push to claim power by assigning great importance to the brilliance of the human race. Nietzsche's idea was that the Enlightenment eliminated any possibility of God existing, so the belief in a Supreme Being was a dead issue in his eyes. There is much evidence of God's existence for disbelievers to study, such as the DNA code. You cannot have a code without a programmer. The World Economic Forum leaders are foolish to make God their enemy, and they will pay dearly for their arrogance.

Nietzsche's philosophy was closely associated with the Nazi movement where Hitler's followers stepped away from moral living and Christian values, replacing kindness with brutality against all enemies. Under the fascists, all useless citizens would be exterminated. The Nazis would go on to purge the population of disabled people, the retarded,

Jews, Slavs, Gypsies, Communists, and anyone who belonged to another political party.

Today the world is going through the same gradual erosion of human rights. Society is bombarded with daily propaganda aimed at vilifying healthy people who do not wish to become experimental pin cushions so that corporate oligarchs can make profits from government contracts. The sales orders for pharmaceutical products are enormous when the public is forced to take the chemicals by coercion and career blackmail. Ironically, the same woke agenda people who are making a fuss about getting rid of oil altogether are the one who promote vaccines and other Western medicines that are manufactured from petroleum.

The two basic emotions are love and fear; all other feelings we know as emotions stem from one or the other. Hatred and jealousy come from a person's subconscious insecurity that someone else will threaten your importance in the eyes of others, or that others will own something which you cannot own. People fear the unknown, so they refuse to accept new ideas that might upset the status quo. It takes bravery to stand up for the truth and to denounce the liars of the churches and governments which they control. If you study the history of the Crusades, you will see how religious wars have destroyed civilizations in the name of religion.

The public is fed a steady diet of fear-based lies via television every day, so that fantasy world becomes reality after constant repetition. The first producer of television programming was Joseph Goebbels, Hitler's Minister of Propaganda. There were a limited number of television sets in Germany during World War Two, so only the inner party members had access to the new visual medium; most of the propaganda went out over the radio, and the Nazis made sure that everybody had a radio at home. The Third Reich parades and gatherings were designed to look spectacular and uplifting; this caused crowds to experience a mass euphoria of patriotism. To enhance the exhilaration further, the

German people were given methamphetamine daily in the form of Hildebrand Chocolates or Pervatin pills. The armed forces personnel were issued Pervatin every day, so they could do battle for three or four days without sleeping.

The drugs allowed the Blitzkrieg tactics to overwhelm traditional armies quickly. The soldiers of France were used to getting a full night's sleep, so they were defeated in six weeks. The evacuation at Dunkirk saved the lives of a quarter of million soldiers.

Adolf Hitler's personal doctor had been giving the dictator various injections of drugs, such as barbiturates to help him sleep and stimulants to keep going during waking hours. In that era, it was legal to have morphine and cocaine. Hitler's ego bloated out of control; he thought he was the messiah so he turned against the churches so that Nazism would become the new religion. Methamphetamine use enabled soldiers to kill without remorse, even though they had been raised in a Christian environment. The notion of going to Hell for eternity did not enter their minds. It boggles the mind how sadistic people can get, yet there is a reason for everything. All the populations and nations involved in the Nazi movement suffered destruction in those countries that had been arguing and fighting each other for centuries. Humans are self-destructive and careless in their actions.

Religious brainwashing over ten years softened the threat of damnation by introducing the doctrines of purgatory and doing the penance handed out after confession to a priest. These are manmade escape hatches constructed out of wishful thinking. Forgiveness is available by praying directly to God, and the condition of being forgiven is that you do not continue sinning. Those who have stolen should repay their victims. The crucifixion and resurrection were a demonstration that God has control over life and death, it was not meant to liberate people from being held responsible for their sins of the past, present, and future. Hell is not going to be a social gathering;

it will probably be a confined state of misery without contact with others.

Those who mock the truth of my words are not worthy of Heaven; they will never hear the voice of God or sense His presence. There are people who long for oblivion, but they will not dissipate or lose conscious thought. The souls who are sent to Hell will become aware that they will never vanish; the fear and torment will never stop. Mankind has been warned about eternal punishment, but there is still much evil in the world.

There is knowledge that I place into my writings about the history of the human race. Mankind is much older than six thousand years. There have been many ups and downs in terms of advancement of the species. Civilizations have risen and fallen on this planet, but God has revealed to me that He created humans on another planet, then moved them to Earth because it had the potential to be a better place for the particular needs of mankind. That means that humans are the real aliens. There are countless other life forms in the universe, and I doubt that more intelligent species would have wars and kill each other as mankind does routinely. It could be that the fallen angels are part of humankind, and their purpose would be to emphasize the difference between right and wrong in a world that is host to God's only son. A soul's character cannot develop in an ideal world where everything falls into your lap automatically. People who have too much of everything without expending any effort become spoiled brats. Lucifer was spoiled as an Archangel, so he decided he wanted to be God in his greedy pride.

The phrase in Scripture that mentions the reason for existence is a clue: "All things were created for him and through him, and in him all things hold together", referring to God's first creation. I am the soul who would also have the function of mediating the energy fields that manifest as physical objects in this dimension. That is the meaning of One God and one mediator, my soul is sort of like a step down transformer known in Physics as the Higgs Bosun, a hypothetical particle that exists simultaneously in every physical manifestation. The physical body is a temporary hub where the consciousness gets organized, but the soul is transitory in nature. The awesome unlikeliness of being the messiah has not been lost on my thinking. It seems infinitely improbable, yet this is the position I find myself in, which is the luckiest soul in the universe.

Isaac Newton calculated the Day of Judgment to happen in 2060 by analysing the many numerical clues in the Bible, but the Last Day could be sooner. God has said that He wants a certain number of souls in Heaven so it will not be underpopulated and boring. It is difficult to imagine what eternity in Paradise will be like, but it is logical that there will be interaction and communication in addition to the reruns of past life experiences available in the memory of each individual. It is a sad fact that many people believe they are automatically saved; they should know that everything in life takes an effort.

There are millions of people who have been brought up in false religions, and they are too indoctrinated to change. The religions that cannot be salvaged include Judaism, Scientology, Jainism, Hare Krishna, Hinduism, Evangelical Christians, Catholicism, and the Church of Jesus Christ of Latter Day Saints. Televangelists, professional prophets, and faith healers will not be forgiven, for they have led many souls astray.

The religions made by men must adapt with the times and stop preaching heresy so that the truth may be revealed. You must never again mention the father, the son, and the holy spirit since those words are blasphemous. It is not enough just to point out the numerous problems of destructive doctrines however, so I will offer the solution. Here is a sermon I suggest that all priests and pastors should present to their church members from now on to save all those of the flock from eternal damnation:

"Brothers and sisters, the coming year is an opportunity to enact shocking changes that will be for the good of all. The human race must

be prepared, because the Judgment could happen in forty years or it could happen forty minutes from now; no one knows but the Father, our God in Heaven. Not even the son Jesus Christ knows the date or time. Centuries of misunderstanding and the buildup of mythology has caused well-meaning organizers of religions to preach things that have been accepted as truths only by way of repetition and general agreement. In this coming year we must apply the real truth supplied by the messenger for the End Times, who is the last rebirth of Jesus Christ. The schemers who seek to hold their positions by clinging to traditional idol worship are throwing away their souls, for some people will never change. Many will continue to pray to other entities besides the one true God who no man has ever seen. It is uncomfortable to do away with lifestyles we have established, but it will be far more uncomfortable to spend eternity in the torment of Hell, so immediate change is necessary. People must stop talking to the emptiness; there is no one who can hear you but Almighty God – no saints, no angels, no ghosts, or spirits are there to hear those prayers. There is no holy mother of God, so it is a grave insult to bestow divine traits to the name of any human Idolatry is not harmless; it is an insult to God."

"Our role as teachers of religion is to teach what is true, not what is invented to attract spiritual tourists so that they will buy the trinkets and statues of religious folklore. Mankind must divest itself of meaningless rituals that have added characters into prayer for the sake of filling the time allotment for gatherings. It would be more constructive to hold musical shows and to provide literature so that people can learn privately, and people should pray in private for the most part. Praying in a concentrated group for a common purpose can be beneficial, but the act of general group prayer usually results in mere regurgitation of phrases that dissipate into thoughtless chants. The Sermon on the Mount tells people to pray by going into your room, shutting the door, and praying to God in secret, so that God will listen, for He hears you in secret. The instruction to pray only to the Father has been tossed by the wayside over many years, so people seek reinforcement by calling on other gods who do

not exist, or by praying to Christ, which is not in Scripture. The function of the son is to warn mankind, to bring the messages of God, and to offer salvation to those who obey God's instructions. God welcomes your prayers of thanks, for He created all of us and He deserves our gratitude always. So do not despair over losing the graven images, the crucifixes, the scapulars, the beads, and the medieval robes of false holiness, for they are only instruments of self-destruction of your soul. Those who partake of idol worship and call on multiple gods will not see Heaven. There will be no amnesty on Judgment Day; there will be no parole from Hell. We must decommission the altars, smash the statues of paganism, throw away the rosary beads, the incense burners, chalices, costumes, crucifixes, scapulars, and other sinful idols that are such an insult to God and his son Jesus Christ."

Congratulations to any brave preacher who will swallow his pride and give my message to the congregation in clear terms. This is no time to hide behind platitudes or speak words about the rapture far in some future scenario erected from the images conjured up by the mysterious phrases in the Book of Revelation. We must spread understanding to those who will listen, for many will desert you when you challenge their beliefs, but do no worry. Remember that when people hate you, that they hated me first. Prophecy says that I would be a man of constant sorrow, quite familiar with pain, despised and rejected by mankind.

John 17:5 *"And now, Father, glorify me in Your presence with the glory I had with You before the world existed. I will no longer be in the world, but they are in the world, and I am coming to You. Holy Father, protect them by Your name, the name You gave Me, so that they may be one as We are one. I am praying not only for these disciples but also for all who will ever believe in me through their words, so that all of them may be one, as You, Father, are in me, and I am in You. May they also be in Us, so that the world may believe that You sent me."*

Creation and Science

People of faith should not denounce all science just because some prominent scientists still cling to false ideas of atheism and Darwinism. A few physicists have made statements about God, but they don't go all the way to insist we must believe that He exists in definite terms due to the pressure of other professionals who might scoff at them. The schools still teach evolution, although there is no fossil evidence that we came from a lower species. The discovery of the DNA code proves that we are highly coded templates. Every code needs to have a programmer to write it, so they cannot say that DNA came together accidentally.

The human species did not even begin on this planet. God said that He moved the human race here because it was best suited to our needs. The original home for humans was in an entirely different galaxy, and there is life throughout the universe. Due to the design of the body, people have to be reborn into the same species rather than to exist in other lifetimes on other planets. The progression of reincarnation causes the individual soul to come back into a new life in a way similar to past lives, hopefully to develop further for the better. God creates new souls from time to time, and all will have a chance to advance in time for Judgment Day. Those who have been victimized will be compensated, and those who have failed obey God's laws will be punished forever. My aim is to save as many souls as possible before the Last Day.

Scientists have found that the physical universe we know has borders that are expanding from the starting point. God created existence by way of a sudden eruption of vibrating energy that brought all things into form, which was the Big Bang of existence. The atheists firmly believe that everything came out of nothing because one day a lot of nothing got tense and exploded, which is preposterous. The Creation had a reason, which is that God felt that it would be interesting to create the conditions for life so that He could observe His living creations share the joy of existence, being connected to all souls.

Before God designed the universe, He created me and named me Yeshua. God realized that there would have to be activity and learning in the scope of consciousness, so that existence would not be boring, but adventurous and interesting. In the beginning of God's plan for creating the material universe, He put together the countless codes, formulas, programs, and streams of energy that would make up all existence. God states that He made life from the raw material of love, which is not a scientific commodity that can be defined in mathematical terms.

To put it simply, everything is made of conscious vibrating energy, and life is a gift from God. Quantum Theory describes matter as concentrated energy that is perceived as solid by an interaction between the consciousness of the sender and that of the receiver, both of whom are observing the wave of matter, thereby collapsing the waves into particle form. All forms exist in energy fields which require a mediator, which is the Christ Consciousness. This matches the phrase in the Bible that "there is one God and one mediator between mankind and God, the man Christ Jesus".

Spiritual exercises such as Yoga, Meditation, and Tai Chi must not be looked on as mysticism, for they are time tested ways to gain insight and peace of mind. Practitioners of Kundalini Yoga learn the discipline of leaving the body, or "soul travelling". The subtle energy known as "Chi" in martial arts seems to run everything. When you concentrate the energy in your body, you can extend your lifespan and achieve physical and mental balance. It is wise to study all available methods of increasing spiritual resilience.

The secret societies who pull the strings hold occult ceremonies to false gods, so it will take some time before a few of them realize that they should be afraid of the real God. This may cause a few elites to defect and turn on their cohorts. If the globalists stay in control, there will be many more tragedies ahead. The current movement to declare a central authoritarian government aims for a world divided into masters and slaves, where dissenters will be censored and cut off from all services. To buy and sell legally under the New World Order, all citizens will have to convert to the one world religion and make the sign of the cross. Most people will be exterminated to reduce the population.

The pope has set up temples and placed himself in the center, so there will be more and more Roman Catholic doctrines gradually introduced into the other religions. This assault on the soul is Luciferian in nature; the Vatican is the Beast, and they should know that those who take the Mark of the Beast will not be allowed into Heaven. It is vitally important to dismantle the Catholic separate school system's theology teaching. Education should be free of brainwashing. Children tend to trust the teachers, so they will believe whatever they are taught. It is only right that they should have access to the truth, not the corrupt pagan doctrines of Trinitarianism and Mary worship. Many Catholic traditionalists will refuse to change, which will be to their detriment on Judgment Day. It takes about two years to brainwash a person, and most children spend over ten years in Catholic schools, so the indoctrination is usually permanently lodged in the subconscious and conscious mind, and cannot be undone without a serious effort by the individual or the work of a skilled de-programmer.

The Catholic church does not believe in the Last Day; they teach that you should have a priest take your last confession and administer the sacrament of Extreme Unction, which is supposed to send you straight to Heaven. Of course, the dying person's family will get an invoice for this service. The church uses the fear of death without the blessing of a priest to control society. In reality, the hocus-pocus of the priest is useless.

Roman Catholicism has taken root in Communist China, a country in turmoil over a universal lockdown. The Chinese government justifies their tyranny using the Covid excuse, even though there is no real threat to human health. In the Orwellian environment of medical fraud and dehumanization, there will be many who comply with the authorities for fear of reprisal. Little by little, freedoms will be taken away until there are just masters and slaves. Bill Gates has been buying up most of the available farmland so that the elites can control the food supply by causing shortages. The upper class manipulators do not care if children starve or if people freeze, they consider those things should be done "for the greater good" of civilization. The elites are fuelled by exotic drugs and perverted crimes against children that would sicken anyone.

High level Freemasons and other secret societies bow to false gods; one is called the Great Architect. There is much anger between religions, and you can tell the worth of a tree by its fruit. The behavior of a person is an indicator of their faith; the groups who engage in violent activity and send messages of hatred out into the world are not very spiritual. Religious intolerance is rampant and promoted deliberately to justify war. The older religions tend to be more peaceful, such as Hinduism. The mystical stories of Hindu tradition seem like fairy tales that have so many deities it's hard to count them all. The only belief system that will save your soul is monotheism, so Buddhism and Hinduism need to be updated in light of newer writings that relate actual words of God. Buddhism has no particular deity and no Scripture from Heaven, while Hinduism has far too many gods on their roster.

It is not difficult to step back and do some self-analysis on the psychology of the things you do to honor God. Karl Marx wrote that "religion is the opiate of the masses", which begs the question of why communism promotes the elimination of religion, since it would be useful in controlling people by sedating their anger. Killing pain with an opiate works by replacing feelings of pain with a temporary fantasy land of pleasure. Everyone has seen religious gatherings where the crowd is whipped into a frenzy of faith by nothing more than some preacher yelling out words with a choir in the background. The people enter into a state of elation, and that gets them through the day. The congregation believes they have demonstrated their faith through reaffirmation, although they have learned nothing from the words of the person holding the microphone. During the week, the trance wears off and the people have to return next week for another fix, so that they can repeat the process of escaping the real world.

The Christian ministers have invested years forming their particular interpretations of Biblical writings, so they will protect their ideas by blocking out any new information that disagrees with them. The media spreads their preaching to the point of no return, so the ones who have avoided actual work by living in the church business all their lives cannot afford to take back their lies and apologize. It may take a new generation to come forward as spiritual leaders who have the intellectual capacity to change that old time religion of superstitious fantasy into a bountiful celebration of truth.

The Scientific Method includes testing an idea experimentally to get evidence of its truth by way of a controlled result. I devised an experiment to test the Scriptural phrase, "Ask and you shall receive, seek and you shall find". I called it "The Prayer Works Experiment", where I would ask for something reasonable during a long morning prayer every Saturday morning for four weeks in a row. My assumptions were logical when choosing my requests in prayer. Praying for four Lamborghini sports cars would never work, since that would be greedy and decadent. It would have to be something modest, so I prayed to God for five dollars, and spent several hours concentrating on the five dollars only. Then I went outside and walked around the city of Ottawa. On all four Saturdays, I found five dollars on the ground just as I requested. That represents a controlled result, so the experiment was a success; I proved that prayer works. Praying to God is a valuable resource, especially keeping a long term prayer about your goal in life.

The elderly nun who informed me I was Jesus in my childhood told me that it was her lifelong prayer to meet Jesus someday, and God granted her request when she was ninety-three years old, so be patient and your sincere prayer will be answered at some point.

In my early days as a wandering musician, I lived many years on the edge of poverty where there was violence and drunkenness. At times was beaten and robbed like a lot of other people, but I kept trying to improve my situation, so that I could live a long a stable existence. I wish everyone success in building stability and security in an environment free of poverty and illness. Being too rich has destroyed people who went too far by cheating and stealing from others, not appreciating that love of money is the root of all evil, and that you cannot profit when you gain the things of this world but lose your soul.

These are the new Covenant rules that churches and their members must follow: no one is to attach divinity to me or pray to me, you must get rid of your crucifixes and statues of Jesus, Mary, and the saints. The priests must decommission their altars and never perform the rituals of blessing holy water and handing out the pagan communion wafers. My body and blood are not hiding in the wine and communion hosts, so the transmutation of my flesh is false doctrine. The churches who engage in heresy and blasphemy are the first ones to call others heretics, while their priests claim to have magic powers. If you refuse to address God as "Allah" in prayer, you will be sent to Hell forever. No one is allowed to pray to Mary or any entity other than God.

It is likely that only a small percentage of Christians will see the light and realize that they must accept the Qur'an as Scripture and change their xenophobic attitudes; others will wait until disaster comes to their doors. Many stubborn people would rather cater to their egos and be sent to Hell than admit they are wrong. The worst group of Protestants I have encountered so far are the Baptists, who express a great deal of hatred and intolerance in their correspondence. None of the Protestant denominations are engaging in any protest against

Catholicism, when they should be concerned that the Vatican wants them dead. Many churches have succumbed to the illegal forced vaccination fear campaign of the Jesuits and had notices on their schedules saying that only those with proof of vaccination would be allowed to attend certain gatherings.

In any system of faith there has to be a state of eternity for all souls where they are either punished or rewarded after the struggle of life in this cruel world. The opposing belief is nihilism, where life is considered to be a meaningless accidental farce with no climax, just a final dark oblivion. Atheists think they will not be punished or judged because they have declared that God does not exist. The atheists are very bad gamblers, for their pride has caused them to bet everything on an empty pot. Those who have misled others into false religions to enrich themselves financially are just as foolish, thinking that God does not know their intentions.

The nations have been fighting with each other for ages, so we should strive for a golden age of secure peace where all people can enjoy the time remaining until Judgment Day. The faithful have no fear of the inevitable end of mankind's physical existence, since it will mean entrance into the eternal bliss of Heaven and freedom from the drudgery of life.

I am the good shepherd; I know my sheep and my sheep know me, just as the Father knows me and I know the Father, and I lay down my life for the sheep. Most of the world's population are disbelievers who will scoff at any such notion of life after death, so they will find the truth after they are sent to be punished forever.

Salvation cannot come from performing rituals, for they only deal with physical manifestations, not the inwardness of the human soul. There is no holiness in sacrifice of living animals because all life comes from God and is therefore precious and should not be interrupted. Being a nice person is a good start, but in light of God's temperament, it is necessary to acknowledge our Creator or else He will not acknowledge you. Thanking God for your existence daily is one way to ensure that you don't invoke His wrath by refusing to cede to His authority through stubborn pride. The boundless pride of man will lead to the downfall of humanity.

Life has moments that are pleasurable enough to remain in the memory as brief thrills of nostalgia over things that have not continued, so those events fade and are ultimately unsatisfactory later in life. In the afterlife, the souls who are pure enough to make it to Heaven will be able to summon up those happy times in great detail at will, which is a valuable prize everyone should be seeking.

There will be various levels in both Heaven and Hell, meaning that reward and punishment will have intensities that are appropriate to the individual after sentencing. The mass murderers and warmongers will re-live the pain of their victims over and over again for eternity. God designs the punishment and the rewards, so all people should be prepared for what is about to happen. There is only one chance, despite the empty promises of commercial religions. The preachers and priests emphasize automatic redemption from sin so that their audiences can feel more secure, but not all those cry "Lord, Lord" will enter the Kingdom of Heaven, only those with pure intentions who do the will of God.

Life is like a river, where the swimmer has three choices: he can swim against the current, he can grab onto a branch and hang on desperately, or he can let go and ride the stream. Most of our lives are spent trying to swim against the current without realizing it. People are raised to

believe that we should struggle to control the environment in order to survive, even

though it is not within our power to dominate all that surrounds us.

Our suffering as a species comes from living in the past through our attachment to memories that then shape our future experiences. The phantoms of past and future are

only useful to the intellect because it gives individuals the notion that they are in control

of their lives. When people grow, they begin to understand that no matter how

strenuously they try to maintain control, life always has a way of changing those plans.

The mentality of trying to force ourselves upon life is the socially accepted norm of

modern civilization. A person's attempt to control life according to his or her own beliefs

includes forcing those beliefs onto others; this is the beginning of tyranny. It is only when you give up forcing and controlling things that you begin to get the kind of control you always wanted but never knew existed.

We do not control our bodily processes, such as digestion, blood circulation, or the

healing of wounds. People who are Naturalists or Humanists insists this complex

existence fell into place spontaneously and evolved from lower species, so I will update

the scientific information on how life came to be and why we exist in the first place. The

discovery of DNA coding is final proof that there was no evolution from primates.

My discoveries in reincarnation caused me to notice that there was a complementary historical figure with exceptional talent who gained notoriety during the lifetime of some of my previous lives, although I am not sure if it is the same person. Michelangelo lived in the same time period as Leonardo da Vinci, Beethoven was alive when I lived the life of Mozart, and Confucius existed as a contemporary of Buddha.

There may be a connection between Michelangelo, Beethoven, and Confucius, but this needs to be clarified to determine if it is coincidental or a pattern of reincarnation. Because life goes on after death, there should be changes made in counselling on death and dying, so that doctors can bring good news rather than doom and gloom to dying patients and their families. Codes of ethics in other areas will be affected for the better by knowing the science of reincarnation. When a prisoner receives a death sentence, the court is actually letting the criminal go, allowing him to reincarnate into someone even more dangerous.

Ethics vary in fields such as medicine, law, politics, and education depending on the general consensus of those involved. Doctors and lawyers are often atheists who have no curiosity about the existence of God since they are busy in their professions. You live, make money, buy a house, raise a family, die, someone else gets the house, and that's it. However, the majority cannot decide there is no God and therefore no divine retribution, because it doesn't work that way. God is not running for reelection at the whim of humans, so everyone who wants to survive must obey His laws. It is a fact that God has appointed me to be the Judge of all human souls, so people should act accordingly and treat others in a decent manner.

Scientists are dependant on their sponsors or schools, so they don't like to go out on a limb by talking about God, although many suspect there is a Supreme Being off the record, which is the same thing as atheism. The least they could do is say a prayer twice a day just to cover themselves, but humans are too proud for that. They can't get rid of me, because God will make sure I keep coming back until I succeed in my mission, so I am passing my warning to everyone that mankind must start pleasing God instead of themselves.

1 John 2:15 *"Do not love the things of this world; if anyone loves the world, the love of the Father is not in them. For all that is in the material*

world – the desires of the flesh, the desires of the eyes, and the pride of life – they are not from the Father but from the world."

Romans 12:2 *"Do not conform to this world but be transformed by the renewing of your mind. Then you will be able to test and approve what is the good, pleasing, and perfect will of God."*

James 1:27 *"Pure and undefiled religion before our God and Father is this: to care for orphans and widows in their distress and to keep oneself from being polluted by the world."*

The reason we are alive is to help each other as we search for God. Having faith in God will lead us to do good rather than evil. Generosity is a running theme in Scripture, for we can all see that greedy people are seldom happy. Humans tend to wallow in misery even though happiness is available through righteous behavior. Tolerance is a virtue that is difficult to maintain in a world that has been divided and set against each other.

There are books and lectures offered by the likes of Neil de Grasse Tyson, Stephen Hawking, and Christopher Hitchens that have sold well to audiences who embrace atheism. Goofy comedians like Bill Maher and George Carlin became rich mocking God's existence when they found that people laugh at religious jokes. Their riches will not help them on Judgment Day; they have misled others into disbelief, and they will not be smiling when they become aware that they are in Hell with no way to escape..

The inner spiritual disciplines of older civilizations and the secrets of the body have been demonized by religions over the centuries, and science is considered heresy to many. Science and faith can now agree, so churches must modernize or disappear under the weight of their myriad mythologies, idol worship, and traditional superstitions.

It is a natural impulse to dislike foreigners who speak a different language and hold opposing beliefs, so it will take work to teach people tolerance. I would advise a person to focus on priorities, especially the fact that your indoctrination may be causing you to act like somebody else, so it is possible to raise yourself above the level of the masses. The focus should be on saving your own personal soul from being sent to Hell.

In Heaven the senses will be amplified throughout a heavenly body form suspended in a field of pleasurable energy vibrations and your thoughts will be widened to have complete memory of all past happy events and feelings which you can experience simultaneously and at will. This is the reward for having a righteous existence when you were in the physical plane. The souls who achieve Heaven will be connected in love; they will be eternally aware of God's presence and they will never be bored. The security and happiness of Paradise will never be taken away.

The preachers and priests do not know much more than their followers, they thrive on guesswork. Certain people believe that they know everything about everything forever, and they refuse to be corrected due to their egotism and pride. Religious groups take in donations and tithes, from which they were supposed to set aside the money so that people would not have to take up a collection when Jesus returns. Instead, they keep all the money for themselves and purchase yachts, Rolex watches, mansions, and jets. Other funds go to set up indoctrination schools to maintain their power and their tax exempt status.

The judgmental ministers and preachers love to throw stones at others, when they should be making themselves useful instead of feeding off their congregations as they proclaim their versions of knowledge. They have used up their Heavenly reward in this life by sponging off of others to get a free ride without doing actual work.

The greed of churches has turned many people against all religion in general, so they become atheists. This break from all thoughts of religion lifts the burden of spiritual responsibility from their shoulders. Avoiding the truth is another form of lying...people lie to themselves and fill in the blanks with personal opinions, feeling that things will take care of themselves. Members of a religion get tied into the social activities and education systems of the church that represents their beliefs. If someone finds the doctrine questionable, they usually do not seek the truth by moving on to another religion, they remain in place hoping for a future correction to happen within their familiar group. Cults maintain their existence through the blind faith of their indoctrinated followers. It is necessary to get all the major religions under the control of a central authority if there is to be a universal doctrine. Today, the world stands on the precipice of doom because that single oligarchy leading the pack of wolves is the Roman Catholic cult. The Vatican holds regular meetings with the leaders of other religions in a step-by-step seduction to the domination of the Vatican and the Antichrist pope.

The planners at the Vatican are in league with the giant banking families of the Rothschild empire. The shylocks who operate the central reserve banks are former Jews who embraced Catholicism and sent their children to various countries to subvert the money supply of vital nations. The central banks are counterfeiters who are above the law: they print money out of thin air, then they loan it to countries at interest. In this manner, the church holds power over those who are indebted to the Rothschild banks.

Millionaire J.P. Morgan was a Rothschild agent and an influential investor who arranged the financing for the construction of HMS Titanic, catering to the fashion craze of trans-Atlantic voyages among the wealthy elite. Titanic was part of the scheme to set up the U.S. Federal Reserve Bank. There were millionaires who were opposed to the creation of The Fed, and some who were in favor of it. The rich folks who were going to vote for the Federal Reserve Act cancelled their voyages on Titanic at the last minute, having been forewarned that the ship was going down. Those opposed to the Fed were still aboard the vessel, and they perished when the ship sunk in 1912. The Federal

Reserve Act was passed the following year, and the United States of America ceased to exist as a sovereign nation.

Catholic bootlegger, racketeer, and investor Joseph P. Kennedy was part of the Jesuit plot; he went on a mission to create a selling panic in 1929, which resulted in the Stock Market Crash and the Great Depression. The stock priced hit record lows, then the agents of the Rothschilds bought up all the companies at pennies on the dollar, thereby gaining control over most industries, especially those who produced armaments and medical supplies. The wars were engineered to bolster the munitions factories and other manufacturers who could produce war materials.

The governments are built on lies just as the Catholic church is built on lies, superstition, and deceit. Trinity worship and idol worship led to the worship of Mary and the veneration of saints. The pope places himself above men and women as if he were divine in some way. Women are considered to lowly to become priests, they must subjugate themselves as nuns and remain celibate. The Vatican has always been a backward feudal institution and it has no plans to change.

A very peaceful sect of Christianity known as the Religious Society of Friends, or Quakers, believe that it is unnecessary to rely on clergy, liturgy, or creed. Quakers are aware that divine essence dwells within us in some measure, and that life is sacred and interconnected. They consider the revelation of God's truth as continuing and ongoing right up to the present day.

Members of the community come together in silence, emphasizing the element of togetherness without rituals or preachers. Each person is capable of direct unmediated connection with God.

Quakers welcome truth from whatever source it may come. When they assemble, it is in a spirit of waiting for inspiration from within. This open minded approach is refreshing, since many other denominations do the opposite by moralizing while preaching fire and brimstone to generate excitement instead of displaying a calm confident faith that never wanes. They do more than talk about being good people; the strength of faith leads to doing good within the community as the byproduct of love for our Creator. Actions speak louder than words. They believe that modelling God's presence in our lives is more important than espousing dogmatic or mystical beliefs.

People who profess to belong to this or that religion often disagree with members of their own group. It is likely that all of them are wrong in their priorities. There is much talk about ancient giants and aliens, but those are petty issues in the face of impending Armageddon. It is important to simplify matters rather than to chase red herrings.

Every person's first priority is to develop a soul that is pure enough to pass Judgment on the Last Day. There is no need to point out the mote of dust in someone's eye if you cannot take the log out of your own eye. No one knows the day or hour of Judgment, so we must be ready at all times.

Western Civilization has been kept in the dark thanks to schools run by the churches; the goal of any church is to obtain money and power, so they keep the public ignorant of certain truths, especially the rebirth of the eternal soul. A rational person would take the concept of reincarnation as good news, yet churchgoers get visibly angry and upset when any truth conflicts with their mental programming. Priests want your money immediately; they want their parishioners to believe this is their only chance to offer money to the church. The member might say he will donate later in another lifetime. The popes had control over the wording of the Bible for many centuries, so there were opportunities to tailor the doctrine to their goal of making the Vatican very rich.

The Anglican faith, known also as the Church of England is similar to Catholicism but without giving allegiance to the pope. Their leader is the Archbishop of Canterbury. The masses are similar, with communion wafers and other sacraments. Although they keep the Second Commandment in their doctrine officially, the communion wafer is very much an idol. The blessing of the cookie does not change it into the flesh of Jesus Christ. Most churches rely on the mysticism of tradition because they do not know the truth. Priests prosper on a litany of lies; they are parasites who are too cowardly to work at a real job. Priests and nuns depend on donations for their housing and food.

The Orthodox churches grew out of the Great Schism. The Russian Orthodox church does not have the pope as leader, but they have retained the trinity and Mary worship. The doctrines and rituals are rife with idol worship icons, relics, robes, crucifixes, Madonna images, and statues.

The first centuries of the powerful church in Rome led to hedonism and corruption. The messiah was treated as God. The cure for the idol worship of the prophet came in the form of the Qur'an spoken to Prophet Muhammad. Islam is one of the world's largest religions, yet the Muslims are divided in theology. The two largest sects are Sunnis and Shiites, both of which maintain the teaching that Prophet Muhammad and Prophet Jesus are two different souls. Muhammad said "*I am all the prophets. I am Moses, I am Muhammad, I am the Final Prophet*". Smaller Muslim groups believe that Muhammad and Jesus (Isa) are the same soul.

The Hare Krishna movement chant to many gods from ancient myth. Jesus says that mere chanting cannot replace eloquent words of prayer and repetitive vocal tones cannot replace intricate original music and lyrics. Those who take part in the Hare Krishna rituals are very nice people, but they worship idols, so their souls are not prepared for Judgment. Idol worship is mortal sin just as calling on multiple gods is mortal sin. Those who are in mortal sin on the Last Day will not be allowed into Heaven.

Buddhism is one of the world's largest religions, with members in Asia and around the world. In North America and Europe many devotees treat the words of Buddha as more of a philosophy than a formal religion. Buddhism has temples and shrines but there is no consensus on how God is defined since the sayings of Buddha did not mention God directly.

Today the Buddhist leader is the Dalai Lama, who teaches that it does not matter whether you believe in God or not. Many intellectuals like the philosophy but declare themselves atheists or agnostics. They do not want a God in their thoughts, and they do not pray. There are people who get interested in Buddhism to find peace of mind and to escape the world.

The person they named as the new Dalai Lama was picked out in childhood, identified as the reincarnation of the last Dalai Lama. The title makes him a dictator over Buddhists even though he is not Buddha. He is a politician like the pope, and the Dalai Lama has regular meetings with the cardinals sent by the Vatican to absorb other religions in the attempt to set up one universal religion, conveniently led by the pope. They are in business together, and their business includes political control.

The pope and the Dalai Lama are now teaching that atheism is fine and that people just have to be nice to each other. Those religions are shell companies that exist to gather money and influence; they are trading the souls of their followers for their temporal goals. Their institutions are not fountains of learning and wisdom, they are brainwashing machines sending people to Hell by releasing them from their spiritual duties to love and honor God.

Faith in God is our ultimate protection from the forces of evil in the long run, but all people should be aware that Satanic forces are at work to take away earthy happiness and all of our God-given freedoms. The wealthy elites grow up as tormented souls, so they lose their morals at an early age. The fathers and grandfathers pass on their hatred of life and their greed for money and power over others. These families breed perverted offspring who become like them; they take part in human sacrifice rituals, sexual depravity, and they are addicted to the exotic drugs of the upper class, such as adrenochrome, cocaine, crack, morphine, and heroin.

There must have been an overwhelming series of events leading up to the cooperation of those in high office who preach crude pseudoscience to justify their actions. Whether through bribery, drug abuse, or blackmail, the civil servants have lost all feelings of pity and human empathy. People will go hungry and homeless because of the endless restrictions on earning a living. The far-reaching medical edicts empower authoritarian governments, not human health. The World Health Organization operates like a global oligarchy, forcing all member states to carry out their orders. Salaried cohorts are too spineless to oppose their bosses for fear of losing their jobs.

History gives clues about the balance of predestination versus free will when we look at events like the World Wars of the Twentieth Century. Both sides suffered enormously, but the Allies ended up winning because they were slightly closer to God. The Nazis had given up on traditional religion to form their own mythical belief system from pagan Nordic legend so that they could eliminate all talk of Jews in religion. Japan's population worshipped Emperor Hirohito as their living god, which enraged the real God, who then caused the atom bomb to be invented so that the balance of power would be in favor of the USA and the war was shortened. Free will has led mankind into conflict so consistently that God allows us to destroy each other temporarily up to a point. Keep in mind that humans create the suffering of others, it is not inflicted on us by God. All those who have died from any cause have been brought back and reincarnated later, so the real damage is spiritual when a person fails to advance in subsequent lifetimes.

The common thinking is that the words in the Bible are one hundred percent correct and not slanted to the agenda of the various men who wrote them down, which is overly presumptuous. Lawgivers and writers of any time period must conform to what society will tolerate officially, such as the topic of gay sex, which would damage procreation and family lineage. Homosexuality was illegal in ancient Sparta was because the ultimate duty of Spartan citizens was to produce more little Spartans who would grow up to become warriors. The Spartans didn't have religious or cultural objections to same-sex relationships and it was a fairly regular practise for married men to have a male consort on the side. The Spartans didn't want any immigrants or outsiders so there was great social pressure to be married and reproduce, but they did not have the same negative attitude toward homosexuality as some people in the modern world do. Now that mankind is in the End Times, there is no pressing need for a larger population, and God does not really care what humans do for sexual recreation as long as you pray to Him daily.

Forcing gay people to be outcasts leads to an underground culture rejected by society, so many people turn away from religion and ease their depression with drugs and alcohol. The basic substance of self-abuse is tobacco, and cigarette smoking is common to those in the gay nightclub scene and those who are habitual drug users. It is written on the packages that smoking tobacco will cause cancer and heart disease, but very few smokers can quit because it is so addictive. Tobacco also saps a person's daily energy and gives their clothes and hair a disgusting smell. Society has been slowly reacting to the enormous medical costs of treating all the cancer cases from cigarettes, which usually ends up with the patient dying after a long and painful period of suffering in the hospital.

The ones who hate the name of Allah are people who speak out of ignorance and xenophobia, so they are not candidates for Heaven because they should know better. Islam is a major religion with millions of devoted followers who are more peaceful than Christians and Jews overall, but Muslims are targets of hate to their competitors. God told me the Jews have lost all favor from Him because of their warlike ways, and He wants Christianity and Islam to unite under the doctrine I give you, which includes Buddhist philosophy. The religions that are not recognized as workable are Judaism, Latter Day Saints, Hare Krishna, Hinduism, Roman Catholicism, Orthodox Christianity, and all other Trinitarian sects.

Muslims must change the beliefs brought about through the Hadith sayings, which are things the storytellers claim Muhammad spoke. The Qur'an does not mention seventy-two virgins awaiting warriors in Heaven, and Allah has said that there is no gender in Heaven. You cannot expect to have a female wife in the afterlife, that is mere gossip. God confirmed that I did not live a full lifetime as Jesus of Nazareth, so the truth is that I left that life before the age of forty.